From Couch
TO CRAZY

**THE MID-LIFE TRANSFORMATION OF A MOM
WHO LOST HER MIND AND STARTED RUNNING**

Erin K. Courtney

From Couch To Crazy

Copyright © Erin K. Courtney (2024)

All Rights Reserved. No part of this publication may be reproduced, stored in a retrieval system, or transmitted, in any form, without prior written permission of the publisher.

ISBN: 9798335273374

The information provided in this book should not be used for diagnosing or treating a health problem or disease, and those seeking personal medical advice should consult with a licensed physician. Always seek the advice of your doctor or other qualified health provider regarding a medical condition. The author and publisher shall have neither liability nor responsibility to anyone with respect to any loss or damage caused, or alleged to be caused, directly or indirectly by the information provided in this book.

Scan the QR Code below for more books!

This book is available at www.amazon.com

-Contents-

Introduction..5

1: A False Sense of Confidence..................................8

2: Ignorance Is Bliss Until It Becomes Misery..............14

3: A Scary Wake-Up Call..20

4: Losing My Marbles...25

5: A Major Breakthrough..29

6: Vacation Epiphany...40

7: From Racing to Quarantine...................................44

8: A New Bike..51

9: Opening the Floodgates......................................55

10: Progress Over Perfection...................................69

11: A Woman's Curse..75

12: Yoda Defeats Hitler..80

13: The Bet..91

14: Homerun Race...96

15: The Nonexistent Parenting Guide...........................102

16: Listening To My Gut...110

17: Mid-life Crisis..118

18: Hometown Half..123

19: Crossing The Bridge...140

20: Elation and Heartbreak..157

21: Go Big Or Go Home...169

22: Reconnecting...174

23: An Unexpected Issue...192

24: Post-Race IBS Flare-Up.......................................201

25: Going Out With A Bang.......................................209

26: The Fountain of Youth is Dry..............................218

27: A New Perspective on Racing..............................231

28: Hitting The Trail...238

29: Weathering The Storm..254

30: Full Circle..263

31: Tomorrow Is An Adventure................................275

32: Old Car Maintenance..281

-Introduction-

Throughout my life when I saw someone out for a run, I would justify why I wasn't out for a run. *I can't do that, running is abnormally hard for me, I just cut my fingernails*; followed by a deep envy of watching that runner so effortlessly pound the pavement. In all reality, I would be huffing, puffing, and wheezing like the Staypuft Marshmallow Man just climbed three steps. Plus, that person was downright **crazy** to run for no reason. No, I would *never* be a runner.

If you had told me ten years ago that I started participating in endurance races in my forties, I would have looked at you like you had an octopus stuck to your face. I'm not an elite athlete; I'm an average mom who would converse with you at the checkout line of the grocery store, a kid's sporting event, or a school dance competition. I blend in with average runners at races, will never break the tape at an event, and I'm happy with that. This book is honest and forthcoming with the physical and mental struggles of becoming a middle-aged athlete with a newfound positive inner voice. It covers my unlikely mid-life crisis; the shift in mindset from fixed to growth. One of my biggest struggles growing up was my internal voice. I seemed cheerful, energetic, and a little obnoxious from the outside. I had no problem encouraging people to live their best lives, but it was different when I spoke to myself internally. My inner voice was negative, condescending, and abusive. Dealing with a voice like that in your head is defeating since you can't escape your mind. If someone talked to me the way my old inner voice did, I would tell them to hit their mute button. For some reason, verbal abuse from within held more weight than it ever should have. It was there to tell me what I couldn't do. Couldn't be. Couldn't accomplish. It told me that I was worthless and pointed out every single flaw I had. Once I started running, it shifted into the voice I used when I was encouraging *someone else*. It became the voice I would use when talking to my best friend, family, or anyone else who is struggling emotionally and needs some positive encouragement and support.

The italicized font is me talking to myself, ***while the bold italicized font is my inner voice, coaching me along this wild ride.*** My inner dialogue between the two shifts dramatically from the beginning to the end of the book and comes full circle.

People tell me, "If you see me running, you better run too because a bear is chasing me!" At first, it was cute and comical, but over time it became so repetitive that my inner sarcasm retaliated. Now, I smile and say, "All I have to do is run faster than *you*," accompanied by a quick wink. Some chuckle at the joke, while others notice the octopus stuck to *my* face.

After having kids, I felt like I lost my identity. I was in Mommy Mode all the time, and working independently from home brought an isolation that obliterated my soul as an extrovert. I didn't have an outlet where I could focus on my interests, and I felt like I needed to support my family by having a flexible work schedule and taking care of things at home. When I started exercising, that was my time to truly feel like myself again and find some personal goals to accomplish. It had given me the energy and stamina to not only keep up with my kids but even challenge them at times *and* do things I never thought I could have done myself.

This transformation has been empowering, showing me that it's never too late to try something new...especially when it's something I *never* thought I was capable of. Now, whenever I doubt whether I can achieve something, I remind myself that I don't know if I don't try.

I have often heard, "I'm just not a runner." I get it because *I* was also not a runner. What changed me? Crossing the finish line, stepping outside my comfort zone, leaving the past behind me, and changing my mindset from fixed to growth. Running is not *just* about running because it has bled over into every aspect of my life. Even if you think running is the devil and think I'm crazy for doing it, this journey goes much deeper.

This book is about stepping outside your comfort zone and trying something new. It's never too late, even if it's small. Baby steps for big babies, as I refer to myself being a big baby. I have no plans to become a star athlete, but the last thing I want to do is look back on my life and wish I had *tried* something that maybe other people (me included) thought was insane and impossible, especially during mid-life. I hope you enjoy this journey and find it as delightful as discovering an extra fry at the bottom of your fast-food bag.

You don't have to be crazy to change the world, but it helps.

-1-

A FALSE SENSE OF CONFIDENCE

October 2012

Standing in the living room holding a hot cup of coffee, I waved out the window as my husband and daughter pulled out of the driveway to leave for the day. David was dropping Kaitlyn off at daycare before going to work, and I was on my own. It was a relief to have a quiet house to myself for a little while.

I thought about how my independence had slipped away after becoming a mom and I had lost myself for what seemed like an eternity. Finding the balance between motherhood and keeping my own identity was far more challenging than I had ever anticipated, and it was a constant battle.

After Kaitlyn was born in 2010, I struggled with *severe* postpartum depression for well over a year. Society told me this was supposed to be the happiest time in my life, yet I was lost in an overwhelming fog of sadness, anxiety, and isolation. I was too ashamed to talk about how I was feeling because I thought that meant I was a failure as a mother. I kept it together on the outside mostly, smiling and laughing around other people, but inside I was completely falling apart. It was obvious to me that I was the problem, but I didn't know how to fix it. A few close friends and family members knew I was struggling but were clueless of the depth and severity of what I was experiencing internally.

It was the lowest, scariest part of my life. Between the roller coaster of emotions from the adjustment of motherhood and loving my baby more than life, to the downs of hating myself so much that I truly believed my daughter would be healthier if I were gone from this world, and she was raised by someone much *better* than me. I felt like I was drowning in a sandpit, gasping for air, yet too afraid to ask anyone for help. I was convinced I had to manage it on my own. I was also hanging on to an extra 50 pounds that weighed on my body, energy, moods, and how I felt physically only amplified my intense depression.

Eventually, I reached a breaking point, and David stepped in to help guide me in the direction of getting the help I needed by going to therapy. As I slowly recovered, I discovered a new depth of empathy for myself and others, understanding that motherhood is complex and perfection wasn't the goal: it was surviving, healing, and learning to have compassion for myself. I emerged stronger over time, not despite my experience but because of it, and I am still standing. Although it was a learning experience, I wouldn't wish for anyone to deal with the emotional turmoil. Unfortunately, my inner voice continued to be harsh and abusive more than I preferred, still wreaking havoc in other ways.

Kaitlyn needs to see you as strong, independent, and the best version of yourself. She also needs to see you here for the family. She needs to see you accomplish everything. It must be perfect, that's your role as a mom.

There is no room for mistakes. She will look to you for direction in her life. Don't screw this up for her, and don't let her see your many flaws. Don't show your flaws to David, either. You don't want him to regret marrying and having a family with you. He is smart and driven; don't keep him from succeeding in his career. He's the breadwinner of the family, so his career is far more important than yours. Your career doesn't matter.

I pushed the negative inner voice aside, smiled at the sun shining on the road, and knew it would be a great morning for a walk before work. I started working from home long before it was considered "cool," and was thankful to have a flexible schedule to balance career and family as a new mom.

I had spent the last two months walking in my neighborhood for exercise and counting calories to lose weight. After meeting with a nutritionist, she suggested that I count my calories rigidly, and limit how much I took in. I could eat a certain amount on my regular days, and little more on days I exercised. I realized quickly when I started counting that it was a *lot* less than I was used to consuming. She said it didn't matter what I ate (although I was constantly getting sick), and to count calories to focus on dropping those unwanted pounds. My weight was slowly coming off, and my energy steadily increased. The better I felt, the better I *wanted* to feel. It was a snowball effect.

Counting calories was my nemesis because it infringed on my love for eating whatever I wanted at any given time, but it also made me realize how much I was *overeating.* Still, my body was adjusting, and feeling better was worth the inconvenience of changing the pesky habits that got me there in the first place.

I was also trying to weasel my way out of maternity clothes since I refused to buy larger sizes due to the weight holding on. Buying larger clothes meant accepting the fact that I was officially overweight and unhealthy, and I wouldn't do it. Kaitlyn was 2 years old, and I couldn't fabricate a good excuse for why I was still wearing elastic maternity pants and stealing David's larger t-shirts because they fit better than mine.

"Please stop stealing my shirts! Every time I know which shirt I want to wear, it's dirty because you took it!" He complained on a semi-regular basis.

"But they're comfortable! And I wash them!"

Although I knew he was right, I was in denial and too stubborn with my refusal to purchase a fluffy-sized wardrobe. Plus, I didn't want to spend the money if I didn't have to. I knew I would *eventually* get back into those smaller clothes.

When I started walking outside for exercise, I quickly noticed that my depression and anxiety had improved. How could jamming out to 90's hip hop while walking in the fresh air and sunshine *not* make even the crankiest person happier? On those walks, I imagined myself lighter and more energetic, dancing around in some of the clothes I so desperately wanted to fit back into. I assumed my husband daydreamed about wearing his own collection of clean, non-stolen T-shirts. How amazing would it be to get out of these stupid elastic pants and oversized shirts to wear some decent clothes again? Yes, please, and thank you.

My middle brother's wife called that morning after she heard about my new walking habit.

"Hey, would you be interested in training to run a 5k next month with your nephew? He's doing the Run Hard program at school and needs an adult chaperone to run with him."

I had heard about the program, working with elementary and middle school kids for 8 weeks to run a couple of days each week after school to train for a 5k race at the end. Andrew was 9 years old, and we hadn't had much time together one-on-one recently, so I also thought it would be a great bonding experience for us.

"Sure!" I replied enthusiastically, though I had never trained for a 5k and had *no* idea what I was doing.

"Okay great! Thank you!"

She was incredibly busy with their three kids, and her options were limited since there was not enough money in the world to pay my middle brother to run. Although Robbie had some allergies as a kid, I was convinced that he was allergic to any form of exercise as an adult. Aunt Erin to the rescue!

When I headed out for my walk that day, I started incorporating short jogging intervals into my routine and assumed it would be a piece of cake. I could only jog for about 20-30 seconds at a time before slowing back down to a walk, but I had to start somewhere. I did as many jogging intervals as I could, with no plan, experience, or knowledge of running. I was nowhere near ready to run 3.1 miles without stopping, but I already felt monumentally better from walking regularly. I had more energy, slept well, and felt better overall. I was neglecting the fact that I had never been a runner, but for some reason, I had a false sense of confidence that I could easily jump into this without much preparation or a real plan to train.

Oh yeah, I'll be ready in a month. How hard could it be to run a 5k with a 9-year-old? It should be easy since I've been walking so much.

Right?

Dressed up for Halloween as Little Red Riding Hood, The Big Bad Wolf, and Grandma. It was the most comfortable Halloween costume I had ever worn.

-2-

IGNORANCE IS BLISS
UNTIL IT BECOMES MISERY

"It's race day!" I exclaimed to David and Kaitlyn as I got up that morning to get ready. My sister-in-law called me a couple of times during the week before, confirming I was still up for the challenge.

Although it was chilly outside, I figured wearing long pants would be a bad idea since I would heat up quickly once the race started. I had lost a little more weight with the so-called training schedule, was more careful about not overeating, and was relieved my own t-shirts were starting to fit again. David was thrilled that I slowly stopped stealing his clothes. However, I didn't have any running pants that fit. It was a choice of wearing pants that were too small that made me look like a penguin on a mission, or in maternity pants too big with my hands grabbing fistfuls of fabric to avoid an imminent wardrobe malfunction. I wasn't particularly thrilled over either prospect.

I decided on a long-sleeved T-shirt and a pair of comfortable exercise shorts, with my regular sneakers to run in. I don't remember what kind of shoes they were because I thought *all* tennis shoes and sneakers were good for running. Having different pairs of sneakers was beyond my comprehension, and I had no idea that developing an addiction to having multiple pairs of running shoes was a real thing. When I got to the race, I met up with my sister-in-law and nephew. The instructions were clear: I had to stay with him throughout the entire route until we crossed the finish line *together*.

"No problem, I'll stay with him the whole way! You ready to do this?" I smiled at Andrew. He smiled back and nodded.

That false sense of confidence was quickly about to catch up to me, but ignorance was bliss at this very moment. We lined up for the race, and the upbeat energy was contagious. Everyone was smiling, happy, and cheering, ready to run.

"Heck yeah, we've got this! We're running our first 5k together, it'll be great!" I exclaimed to him.

The horn blew, and the excited kids took off with squeals, going way too fast for a run that was 3.1 miles long. Andrew was all smiles as we jogged along with another friend of his accompanied by his dad, who was in *much* better shape than me. Less than a half mile in, I struggled to catch my breath and slowed down significantly. Andrew looked back, signaling me to keep up with him.

"I'm trying!" I cried out and picked up the pace a little...but it didn't last long until I started breaking down again.

You can't do this. This is too hard. Why are you even here?

His friend's dad saw me, then slowed down and asked, "Are you okay?"

"Yeah, this is a lot harder than I thought it would be," I admitted, desperately trying to catch my breath.

"He can run with us if you need to slow down. We'll stick together the whole way."

"Are you okay with that?" I asked Andrew.

"Yes!" he replied, excitedly.

He wanted to stay with his friend and keep going instead of hanging back with his out-of-shape aunt. I smiled at Andrew, nodded to the dad, and immediately slowed down to a walk while I watched them jog ahead, quickly disappearing into the crowd. My heart sank.

Did you seriously think you could run an entire 5k without stopping? What were you thinking?

Yes, I did. I thought I could do this because I didn't think it would be that big of a shift to go from walking to running. I was wrong.

You're terrible at this. Absolutely awful. And you're letting your family down because you promised you'd stay with him the entire way. What if something happens to him and you're not there? You would never forgive yourself. You should be ashamed.

I continued to walk and watched as people passed by me like I was standing still, and I felt like a failure. I tried jogging a few more times along the route, but only made it about 10 seconds before I had to slow down to a walk again and gave up running.

You are a pathetic disappointment to your family and yourself.

I accepted my failure and continued to walk, wishing the route would end quickly because I was physically, mentally, and emotionally miserable. It felt like it was taking me three hours to finish with how slowly it went by, and the abusive thoughts constantly chimed in about how terrible and awful I was. After what felt like an eternity, I heard cheering up ahead.

YES! The finish line is getting closer!

I started walking faster because I needed anything to get through this mess. It sucked, and I wanted to go home. I was more miserable mentally and emotionally than physically and wanted to cry right there on the course, but I had to bury it deep down inside. After rounding a corner, I saw it up ahead.

Okay, I have to run through the finish line.

Adrenaline kicked in, and I took off at a sprint that immediately slowed down again once I felt the wheezing in my lungs and burning in my legs. I didn't let up completely with running, since I wanted to at least *jog* through the finish line. It was a miserable struggle; I didn't know my exact time and certainly didn't care.

Andrew, his parents, and both little sisters Rachel and Emma, were waiting for me at the finish line along with a few other extended family members. My sister-in-law snapped a picture of me coming in and then asked why I didn't stay with him. I hung my head and explained what happened. I was embarrassed and devastated that I couldn't follow through with what I was specifically there to do.

"It's a good thing he was able to run with his friend and another adult," she said. I agreed and apologized again.

In front of my brother's family, I fought back tears over the disappointment and feeling like a failure because I didn't follow through with the commitment and let them down.

You should have known you wouldn't be able to run that entire race and cross the finish line with him. You can't run long distances.

When I got to my car, I broke down into a heavy sob, and my shoulders shook with every deep breath. It was an overwhelming release of emotion that I had been holding inside, and there was a mix of relief and exhaustion in the sobbing, as though I finally permitted myself to feel the depth of sadness in the moment. As a child, I was ridiculed for crying and built up a tough shell that prevented other people from seeing my vulnerability, and it carried into my adult years with only crying in private when no one else could see me. After the sadness was released, it quickly turned into anger, then my inner voice started rationalizing why I never should have committed to this race.

Who do you think you are? You're not a runner. It's ridiculous that you promised to do something that is impossible for you to do. You're overweight, in your thirties, and if you couldn't run a mile in high school you certainly can't do it now. Or ever, for that matter. Being a runner is an unrealistic dream for you. Get over it and stick to what you know.

The flow of negative self-talk was overwhelming as I took it all in and listened to it dominate my thoughts and continued to cry. I felt helpless, like I was curled up in a ball and being kicked while I was already down.

Don't waste your time trying to run. You'll never be able to do it.

On the outside I looked normal, but on the inside I was an emotional dumpster fire.

-3-

A SCARY WAKE-UP CALL

"Are you ready to go see Grammy and Grampy at the beach?" I asked Kaitlyn as we were packing up a month later.

"Yes!" she squealed excitedly.

I grew up in Surfside Beach, South Carolina, where my parents lived at the time, and we always looked forward to visiting them for a weekend. David was immersed in a big renovation project, completely rebuilding our back porch, so those weekend getaways gave him extra time to work on it. Meanwhile, Kaitlyn and I enjoyed spending time at the beach with my parents, making it a perfect arrangement for all of us.

My dad's family had a big reunion planned at the Myrtle Beach State Park, bringing together many relatives I hadn't seen in years, most traveling from out of state. David is an introvert, so avoiding a massive number of strangers to hunker down and focus on a project at home was right up his alley while being at the beach to socialize was my happy place. We are the perfect example of yin and yang.

The reunion was held in a large shelter near the park's entrance, bustling with cars coming and going. It was nice outside, even though it wasn't summer. It wasn't warm enough for short sleeves, but it also wasn't cold enough to be stuffed into a parka. The park was busier than usual since the weather was so pleasant and many people were on their Christmas Break.

There was a Cornhole game set up, and several people had gathered around to start playing a mini-tournament. My dad's cousin is very competitive and a big trash-talker, so the sarcastic banter started immediately when I walked up to play against him.

"I just want to let you know that I don't take it easy on women," he said to me.

"That's fine, I don't take it easy on men, either," I retorted with a smirk.

His face dropped from shock, then smiled when the surrounding family members laughed at him.

"Oh, I *like* you! This will be a fun game!"

The banter went back and forth as we played. I liked to play Cornhole for fun, but a fire was ignited in me from the challenge. It was a close game, and I was *lucky* to win...but I didn't care. A win is a win. The family erupted in cheers when my dad's cousin lost to a woman, and I couldn't help but chime in.

"I took it easy on you since you're *old*," I smiled.

"Ahh!" he cried, then lit up into a laugh.

"Good game, I'm going to help set up the food. You know; my *womanly* responsibilities," I winked.

"I want a rematch!"

"I'm leaving on a high note!" I laughed as I walked toward the shelter to set up the desserts I brought.

A few years prior, I created a recipe for an Oreo Trifle after digging around the internet, unable to find one. This recipe had become one of the signature desserts that regularly came with me to any gathering for a good reason. Layers of rich chocolate fudge brownies, chocolate pudding, milk-soaked Oreo cookies, and whipped topping made it a crowd favorite.

Kaitlyn was with my mom and two other aunts while I was helping set up food in the shelter. One of my favorite things about family gatherings is the massive amount of grub because we love pigging out. I couldn't wait to dig into the buffet in front of my eyes. As I chatted with family members, I suddenly heard screams.

I looked over and saw my little girl running towards the busy main road, my mom and aunts chasing after her and screaming in a panic for her to stop. Kaitlyn thought it was a game and giggled as she ran faster, unaware of the danger ahead.

I was about 100 yards away and took off at a full sprint, focused on my baby headed for the road of oncoming cars. Other family members cried out, but no one was close enough to catch her. My arms and legs pumped hard as I flew past my mom and aunts like they were turtles sunbathing on a log. My vision was laser-sharp and focused on her as I ran faster than I ever thought was humanly possible for my body. At that moment, I transformed into an Olympic sprinter, driven by pure panic. Just before she got to the traffic, I was running so fast that I slid past her into a pile of pine straw like I was sliding into home plate and almost into the parked cars by the road.

She jumped with surprise when she saw me, then squealed with delight and ran in the opposite direction, directly into my mom's arms, smiling back at me. I sat there in the pine straw, processing what happened, looking back at the busy road, and the questions inside my head came flowing out like a tsunami.

Why did she take off like that? What if I hadn't gotten to her in time? Would she have kept running? Would one of those cars hit her and destroyed our family's life??

I shook my head in disbelief, got up, brushed myself off, and walked back over to her. I took her from my mom and wrapped my arms around her.

"Baby, you *cannot* take off like that, you could have gotten hit by a car!" I said. Her eyes got big as I pointed to the traffic she almost ran into.

"Oh!" she exclaimed.

She had never done that. This was the child who would cling to whoever was close by because she was too scared to venture off on her own. I hung my head and felt myself choking back tears over the "what ifs" that almost happened in front of my eyes. We had come so incredibly close to disaster.

I had a sudden realization: *my regular exercise paid off in a way I never could have anticipated.*

Even though I wasn't running anymore, staying active had kept me fit enough to move quickly when it mattered most. I didn't need to be a star athlete, just capable of moving in an emergency. The regular movement and weight loss had put me in a position to go when I *really* needed to, and this situation called for quick action. She might have stopped before reaching the road, but she might not have. It hit me with an overwhelming force of how much I appreciated being able to take off at that moment.

Kaitlyn, age 2.

-4-

LOSING MY MARBLES

...ALMOST TEN YEARS LATER...

"Hey, I'm going to run the Riverbanks Zoo 5k next month. You want to come with me? It's a walk-friendly event if you don't want to run," David asked.

He was a runner on and off through his thirties but had gotten back into it and was looking at some local races for motivation. He's one of those people who can go a year without running, then bust out 3 miles like nothing happened. He makes me sick with those insane genetics. I had spent the last few months consistently walking about 3 miles per day, 4-5 days per week. It was April, and the weather was perfect (minus the pollen). Completing the distance wouldn't be an issue at all if I was *walking* but I had completely given up on running.

After giving birth to our son in 2015, we happily said, "Two and through!" with having kids, so we closed up shop in the baby-making mill. Our family was complete when Alex was born, and I had packed on some more weight. Two years later, I was diagnosed with three digestive disorders and an autoimmune disease. The medications did nothing to help how sick I felt all the time, so I was forced to change my diet.

Although I was a giant baby about making any changes, it paid off in the long run. The weight had come off slowly, but I felt exponentially better, and the extra 50 pounds melted away over time.

"Yeah, that sounds like fun!" I exclaimed.

"Are you going to run or walk?"

"You know, maybe I'll try to start jogging. I've never run an entire 5k before."

"Here's the perfect opportunity to do it!"

I smiled as I daydreamed of the *impossible*; running for three miles without stopping. I had forgotten about the 5k I did ten years prior. It's amazing how we tend to "forget" some things...or maybe block them out. Either way, my original commitment to this race was to complete it by myself; I didn't have to run or be responsible for another person. Maybe most "normal" people wouldn't consider doing a 5k in any fashion to be fun, but the thought of a race going through our local zoo was different. The walk-friendly events didn't pressure you to go fast, there would be plenty of scenery to look at along the route, and many other people would be walking as well. We were also able to explore the back side of the zoo that only the employees got to see, and that was intriguing as well.

Okay, you can walk this event for sure, but what if you trained to jog? You have less than three weeks. No pressure, you don't have to jog the whole way, but you can try.

Oh boy, there goes that voice in my head again.

Although it had been there throughout my life, it wasn't positive very often. It was usually there to put me down and tell me what I couldn't do. Ask me why I'm trying to do that when it's just a waste of my time. It reminded me that I wasn't good enough and never would be, and I had accepted it. However, I noticed that when I started walking regularly, the voice slowly became a little more positive. So, I started doing what I had done ten years prior: added short jogging intervals to my walking routes. I didn't jog much, just little spurts where I could squeeze it in, and my body could handle it. I started with 20-30 second jogging intervals, slowed to a walk until I was ready to jog again and repeat. Although I had heard about "Couch to 5k" training programs, I didn't research them. I winged it while listening to my body and did what I could when I could. It felt simple.

I knew that even if I couldn't run the whole 5k, this would at least increase my chances of being able to do so. Again, there was no pressure this time around. I didn't have to keep up with anyone else, it was something to accomplish on my own; for myself. I wouldn't be letting anyone else down. It was different. I was doing it for *me*, which I hadn't done much for myself for years.

Although I did jog intervals, I spent those 2 ½ weeks focusing mentally on being able to walk the event instead of running. While I felt my endurance improving a little bit each time I went on my route, I wasn't hard on myself about running. My mind was calm, pleasant, and peaceful while training, and I had a good feeling about the race.

Maybe it will be different this time.

No caption is needed, the pic says it all.

-5-

A MAJOR BREAKTHROUGH

"Are you ready?" David asked as we rode in the car to the Riverbanks Zoo the morning of the 5k.

"Oh yeah, I can cover the distance walking, no problem."

"Aren't you planning to run it?"

I sighed, "Yeah, maybe. If I can."

"What do you mean if you *can*?"

My mind flickered back to the last 5k from ten years ago, and I seriously doubted whether I could run the entire distance without walking. I hadn't done it in my training and it still seemed impossible. It felt like I needed more time.

"I don't know, I'm just not sure I can run the whole distance without slowing down to walk. I've never done that before, and I'm almost 42 years old. I'm not a natural runner like you are."

"Pfft. If you automatically tell yourself that you can't do something, you're setting yourself up for failure. Just plan to run the whole thing and *do* it!"

Bless his heart, thinking that everyone can run like he can. I don't think he realizes that he might be partially immortal for that reason alone.

I agreed and told him that I would try my best. He nodded in approval as we rode together listening to the radio. I wasn't stressed about the race; I was going out there to complete the distance and see what I could do. Couldn't run the whole way? No big deal, it would be a new and fun experience. We arrived and parked in the extended parking lot. A chunk of the race route was in the main parking lot, so we had to park farther away and cross the walking bridge to get to the main entrance. As soon as we got to the walking bridge, you could hear the volume steadily rising of music and people. Everyone had arrived in their running gear with race bibs attached to their shirts, making their way to the front. The energy was infectious, and I started to get excited.

"I LOVE the energy!" I cried as we walked to the start line and was bopping along to the music playing.

I headed for the restroom to empty my bladder before the start, and although the line was as long as it was at the DMV, it moved rather quickly. I stared in awe at the people you could tell were serious runners. They were obviously immortals.

I'm staring at centaurs up close.

We lined up behind the runners at the start line when David asked me, "Should we be closer to the walkers since we're not serious runners like them?"

I looked around at the crowd as we stood on the edge and replied, "I think it's okay, we're behind the fast people, and we're also way off to the side so anyone can pass us easily. We're out of the line of fire."

He shrugged, and we moved farther over to the side to avoid the stampede once it started. The horn blew, and everyone took off. We stayed over to the side and stuck together for the first minute, taking it all in and moving along at a steady pace. Then, he looked over at me and smiled.

"Ready to speed up?"

"Uhh, *no*. You go ahead, there's no way I can keep up with you."

"But I thought we were doing this together?"

"Dude. I can *NOT* keep up with you. You don't understand. Go ahead, see what you've got! I don't want to hold you back!" I fussed.

He still didn't get it.

"Are you sure?"

I rolled my eyes and huffed, "Am I going to tell you to do something if I don't want you to do it?"

"No, you wouldn't. Okay, I'm going to go."

"Good! GO! See you at the finish line!" I shooed him away with my hands and flashed a big smile.

We both had goals to accomplish and maybe one day we would run together...but that was not the day. He smiled back at me, faced forward, and picked up his pace. I watched as he inched farther and farther away until I couldn't see him anymore going around the twists and turns of the route.

Okay, let's do this. keep a steady pace.

Oh hello, there is that voice. It's quite encouraging today; unlike the last 5k I did. That's a pleasant surprise.

There were many photographers on the course, and I gave a big cheesy grin at each one I saw as I heard the *click* of the camera. I wore a funny T-shirt and was proud of my choice for the pictures. It was a shirt that was making fun of exercise *and* talking about food, so it was extremely appropriate for the occasion and the person wearing it.

The course was beautiful. Although we had been

to the zoo many times over the years with our kids, this was a completely different experience running through it, and without any whining or complaining from them about how they were hungry, wanted to see the monkeys, or they might collapse if they didn't get ice cream. It was peaceful, pleasant, and even more enjoyable than I anticipated. The twists and turns through meticulous landscaping and shaded paths with different animals to look at were so much fun to experience. From the kangaroos and rhinos to the giraffes and zebras, the scenery was exquisite. After finishing the interior route of the zoo, we made our way to the bridge over the Saluda River which was the halfway point. My lungs burned, my legs ached, and I was getting very tired.

I was just about to give in and slow down to a walk when I heard someone say to the person next to them, "Hey, we're almost halfway through!"

Wow. Really? Are you telling me I've jogged almost a mile and a half without stopping? I've never done that before!!

Imagine what it will feel like to make it to the finish line without slowing down to walk at all. Wouldn't that be great?

Oh wow. Yes, that would be fantastic. Amazing. Phenomenal. It would be a first!

Don't give up; stay steady and keep going.

Okay, let's see how far I can go.

As I followed the route, I saw the curve as we ran along the back side of the zoo where only the employees were allowed. Now *this* was cool, just because it was a part of the zoo I had never seen and felt like we had special backstage passes at a concert. I slowly started to come up behind a man who looked like he was my dad's age, jogging along the route.

Oh, I can't wait to tell my dad that people are out here running who are his age.

However, the excitement turned to concern as I got closer to him. Although he was moving along steadily, his breathing sounded harsh, like he was struggling to breathe. I looked around and saw a few people up ahead and a couple more behind us.

He doesn't sound well at all. Do I have my phone? Yes. Maybe I should stay with him in case something happens.

I slightly slowed my pace to stay behind him, listening and watching as we jogged along. His pace was steady, and although I thought his breathing sounded off, it was consistent. He had no idea I was right there; he was focused on running. I looked back again and saw a few more people getting closer. After staying with him for a few minutes, it eased my mind and I figured he would probably be okay since he seemed content and steady, chugging along. I kept my ears and eyes peeled and looked at him as I slowly passed. I could see it on his face and in his body language that he was focused and determined, and I felt even better about moving ahead.

Suddenly, I smelled something strong. *Really* strong, and quite unpleasant. I'd always had a powerful sense of smell, and it's been both a blessing and a curse. For good smells like chocolate chip cookies, ocean air, or a campfire, it's heavenly. For bad smells like body odor, gasoline, or rotten food, it's borderline torture. I looked ahead and saw something that looked like a large pile of dirt...only it wasn't dirt.

Is that what I think it is?? Is it a huge pile of animal poop?!

Several people around me noticed it too, and I started laughing.

"That makes the route more interesting!" I cried.

We all laughed as I tried desperately to "ignore" the smell. I couldn't exactly hold my breath while running, because that didn't seem like the greatest idea in the world. I huffed and puffed along, trying to get past it as quickly as possible when a thought hit me.

Am I breathing in POOP particles???

The thought alone made me laugh out loud again, trying to entertain myself as much as possible while running past it. Distraction has a way of making you forget what you're struggling with in the moment. The next thing I knew, I hit mile 2.

Look at that, you only have a little over one mile left to run. You've already run two; you can make it one more.

Oh wow. Is this possible?

Yes! It IS possible. Keep going!

I realized that I might be able to run a 5k all the way through without stopping. I felt the adrenaline surge and I was determined to keep trying.

You can do this. Stay steady. You don't have to run or sprint, just keep jogging.

My lungs are screaming at me to walk. I'm tired. My legs hurt. I don't think I can do this.

How incredible would it feel to achieve something like this for the first time in your life? In your forties??

But I'm so tired. I just want to walk.

Don't you want to be able to accomplish running a 5k without stopping?!
YES! Yes, I do!!!
We rounded out the last part of the course that was inside the zoo, then went through the gates of the parking lot for the last leg of the route. The finish line was less than a mile away.
This is it! Keep going! Just a little bit farther! Don't give up!
Okay, I've got this! Complete the circle in this oversized parking lot and the finish line is at the end!
The sun was beating down on the asphalt, draining every bit of energy I had left in my body...but I was almost there. The finish line was so close.
Look! There it is! Just circle one last time, maybe a quarter mile left!
Oh my gosh, I am beyond exhausted. I think my legs are going to fall off. My lungs burn. I'm so thirsty. I'm sweating like a pot-bellied pig desperately looking for a cool mud puddle and probably smell like one too.
LOOK AT HOW CLOSE YOU ARE!!
Okay, that's it! I just passed mile 3, so that's only one-tenth of a mile left to go!
I heard the beeps ahead of each person running through the finish line, with their race chips recording their time. I couldn't believe how close it was and that I had actually been running the entire time.
This is it!! GO!! You've got this!!!
I saw David standing just ahead of the finish line, holding his phone and taking a video of me coming in.
When I saw him, I yelled, "I ran the WHOLE way!!!" with my arms up in disbelief.

"All right! Good job!!" he cheered.

There it is! Keep going! You're almost there!!

I ran through the finish line and heard the beep of the timer go off, and a flood of emotions came billowing through like nothing I had ever experienced.

I RAN THE ENTIRE 3.1 MILES WITHOUT STOPPING OR SLOWING DOWN TO WALK!!!

I wanted to laugh. I wanted to cry. I wanted to jump up and down and squeal like that sweaty pig looking for its mud puddle. I also wanted to lie down in that cool mud puddle to rest, but the adrenaline and emotional high of completing something I thought was impossible for me was too much to do any of those things other than stand there in shock with a big, goofy grin plastered all over my face.

YOU DID IT!!!!

After the race, we walked around and did some light stretches while drinking water. The feeling was a dopamine high, unlike anything I knew. My right hip flexor felt a little tweaked at the end, but overall, I felt good. The emotions at this point far surpassed any fatigue, and I was beside myself with pride and joy.

"How did you do?" I asked him.

"Pretty good for my first race getting back into it, but I made a mistake and pushed too hard when I shouldn't have," he said with a smile.

"Why, what happened?"

"Someone pushing a stroller with a baby passed me, and I took off. I can't let a *stroller* pass me."

I laughed, "You're ridiculous. You know how much they probably train pushing that stroller, right?"

"Yeah, I know."

My motivation increased tenfold, realizing that I could do this. Training would be better. My mindset was better and more focused. I *could* do this when I was so convinced I *couldn't*.

You're almost 42 years old and just ran your first 5k!
THIS CHANGES EVERYTHING...

"There's a half-marathon nearby this November, and I'm going to sign up for it. Do you want to do it too?" David asked that afternoon while searching for more races. He was already hooked.

Yikes, a Half-Marathon? That's 13.1 miles!!! And I struggled through a 5k this morning, which is 3.1 miles! Another TEN miles?? Am I capable of doing something like that so soon?

"We just ran a 5k a few hours ago! I don't know, a Half-Marathon seems like a little much for me starting out," I immediately said with doubt and skepticism.

"Come on, Erin, go BIG!! You can do it; I believe in you! We can do it together!"

This man has lost his marbles.

I laughed, "We might be able to be at the same race together, but there's no way I could run with you right now. That's my dream one day, to be fast enough to keep up with you."

"You could keep up with me now, you just gotta push harder!" he teased.

"Yeah, I could keep up with you on a *bike!*"

That would be incredible to be fast enough to keep up with him. He's so far ahead of me.

You will run with him one day; stay consistent with your training, be patient, and give it time.

I was completely in love with the shift of the new inner voice. The new Yoda voice was very refreshing compared to the old Hitler one.

Realistically, you won't be able to keep up with him in a Half-Marathon in five months, but you could certainly train to complete it. You don't know if you don't try. Let's at least start training for it.

Okay. I want to try.

I took a breath and said, "I'll do it."

"Great! I just got us registered!"

After I posted a picture on social media from the 5k that morning, I received a phone call from a longtime childhood friend.

"Hey, I saw you did your first 5k, that's so great! I'm doing an all-women's Sprint Triathlon in August; you should come with me and do it too!" said Skibner.

"You're doing a *triathlon*??" I gasped.

"Yep! It's a sprint triathlon, so it's a 250-meter pool swim, an 8-mile bike ride, and a 2 ½ mile run. Start training so you can come with me, we'll make it a girls' trip!" she said.

"That's so awesome you're doing this!"

"You can do it, too!"

I laughed, "Yeah right, that's insane!! I could *never* do a triathlon."

Beyond ecstatic, and slightly goofy.

-6-

VACATION EPIPHANY

"WHO'S READY TO GO TO THE BEACH?!?!" I squealed at my family on a Sunday morning as we were packing up our luggage. The kids squealed back in excitement, and my reserved husband even cheered along with us.

Every summer, we take a week-long vacation to Pawleys Island, South Carolina, with David's family. When I refer to family, this includes aunts, uncles, and cousins that usually end up being about 25 people. We used to all fit in one big house when there were 18 of us, but as we started reproducing the numbers grew. This led to renting two houses, but we still gather regularly during the week.

He loaded up the car while I was double-checking the house to make sure we didn't forget anything, although I knew this was fruitless because someone always forgets something on *every* trip. The previous year, we were given complimentary bike rentals along with the house rental, and we were smitten with riding bikes in the area all week. David is tall and looked like a hunched-over turtle riding a Granny bike the previous year, so we decided to bring our bikes with us.

Our bikes weren't special. They were 15-year-old basic mountain bikes we bought on a limited budget before having kids. However, they were *our* bikes, and we wanted to ride them while on vacation. As an adult, the same thing comes flying out of my mouth every time I get on a bike and start pedaling.

"I LOVE riding bikes!! We need to do this more often!!" I yell with enthusiasm as I start pedaling ferociously, leaving the family in my dust until they fuss at me to come back. I'm pretty sure I won't receive a Mother of the Year award with my "Leave them in my dust" attitude, but I digress.

Growing up in the 80's and 90's, I practically lived on my bicycle spending time outside with friends. Hopping on a bike and pedaling immediately takes me back to that time of a carefree life, feeling the breeze on my face with my hair flying behind, and the sound of the pedals and wheels turning. The next day, David and I went out for a morning ride and rode about 4 miles before he was ready to head back to the house.

"My butt hurts from this seat, it's brutal!"

"I'm going to keep riding for a while, I'm not ready to go back yet," I said.

David talked me into getting a watch to track mileage and heart rate with different workouts, and I immediately fell in love with it. My new watch was tracking mileage, so I turned on some music that blasted through my phone in my pocket and kept riding. As time passed and my legs finally started to tire, I looked down at my watch and gasped. It had recorded that I rode TEN MILES!!!!

What?! Is that accurate? How did I go that far??

I rode back to the house since the pain was starting to settle in from my lousy seat. I assumed I lasted longer than David because I have more cushion on my body than he does. Just then, my inner voice came flowing into my head.

You just rode ten miles, can run a 5k, and you know how to swim. That's a triathlon...

It was like a lightbulb lit up as bright as the sun over my head. The Almighty Yoda Voice in my mind had spoken; I was going to start training for my first sprint triathlon in two months for the She-Tris All-Women's event in Mount Pleasant!! When I got back to the house, I carefully peeled myself off the bike and felt like I had been riding a horse for three days straight. My saddle area was toast, and I immediately called Skibner to tell her the good news.

"YES!! We'll take a girls' trip together! This will be awesome; you will love it!" she cheered.

After waddling up the stairs like a duck, I frantically looked for David to tell him the wonderful news. My legs still felt like noodles.

"I'm going to do my first triathlon in August!"

"Wait, *what*?"

"It's the one Skibner told me about that is for women. It's a sprint race and will be perfect for a first-time event! I can practice swimming in the pool and ride my bike in the neighborhood! It'll be awesome!!"

"Okay. Be sure you know what you're getting yourself into."

There's nothing holding me back now. It's time to start swimming...

Oh, and I should probably get a new bike. I can't imagine bringing my old hunk of junk to a triathlon.

*Alex showed us the correct way to eat ice cream while we were on vacation. Apparently, I had been eating it incorrectly by getting it **inside** my mouth.*

-7-

FROM RACING TO QUARANTINE

When I woke up the morning of the Born In The USA 4-Miler race on the 4th of July, something felt off. My head hurt and I was tired but felt well enough to run. I chalked it up to the summer cold I was developing that was passed along from Alex and didn't think much of it. I ate a light breakfast, loaded up with water, and drove to downtown Columbia for the event.

I pulled up in the parking lot and grabbed a good spot near the start, early enough to stretch and wait in line to potty before it began. Using a port-o-potty had become my nemesis after a traumatic experience years ago when I had to use one with poop smeared all over the walls, and that was the fastest I have ever peed in my life. Although I'm still not a fan of using them, it's better than peeing all over *myself* during a race.

I took two last sips of my water before hopping out of the car, stuffing my key fob and phone in my pockets. The serious runners were warming up in the parking lot, doing sprints and stretches. I loved watching them, it was like I was a spectator looking at immortal creatures with wonder and amazement.

Centaurs.

Even my inner voice saw these people as being immortal. I walked around, looking for Skibner. She was doing the relay part of the race and partnered up with another person so they could each run 2 miles.

You know you can run a 5k and have spent the last two months training, so running 4 miles shouldn't be a problem. Do what you did before and keep going.

Skibner was nowhere to be found, so I called her.

"Where are you? It's starting soon!"

"I'm doing the second leg of the relay, so I have to wait at the halfway point!"

I looked around for someone that I knew but had no luck. Being so new to the running world, I hadn't met many people yet, and I waited with the crowd for the race to start. Many people were dressed for the holiday, wearing red, white, and blue. I chose another funny shirt that was color-coordinated for the holiday.

I felt pretty good during the first two miles, just kept it steady and jogged along. It was a beautiful part of downtown Columbia through Forest Acres, so I took in the scenery. At the 2-mile point, I saw people waiting for their relay team members to get there so they could take off. I kept looking for Skibner but didn't see her. As I went around the curve, I slowed down and noticed that something was amiss.

Just keep going. You're feeling very off but stay steady. You've got this.

Something doesn't feel right. I'm abnormally worn out, and my heart rate is higher than usual while running. That's weird. What's going on?

Keep going but don't push too hard.

As I approached mile 3, I saw someone familiar ahead and couldn't help but pick up a little speed. When I got closer, I raised my hand in the air. Just as I was passing her, I brought my open hand down and slapped her hard on the butt, shouting, "GO SKIBNER!!!! YOU GOT THIS GIRL!!"

She almost jumped out of her skin and swatted at me, but I jumped out of her reach and cackled.

"Good lord, you scared *me!*" cried the man running next to us.

"I'm sorry, I couldn't help it!"

"That's okay, it's been the most entertaining part of the race so far! Thank you!"

"Well then, you're welcome!"

We continued along the route for another quarter mile, talking about how ridiculously hot and humid it was, and how both of us were struggling immensely.

"Go get it!" she yelled as I started to break away.

"See you at the finish line!"

Fortunately, the last part of the race had a slight decline, so I didn't have to fight running uphill. I was extremely worn out and couldn't escape the nagging feeling in my gut that something was wrong.

Don't stop now, you're super close. Almost done. Look, there's the finish line!

I saw it up ahead, and although my mind was full of excitement, my body was not. I picked up the pace a tiny bit; unnoticeable to anyone other than me. My legs and lungs burned tremendously running through the finish line, hearing the beep of my racing chip recording the time.

Wow, that was a lot harder than I thought it would be today. I'm so glad it's done.

I waited at the finish line for Skibner to come through, ready with my phone to take pictures. When she finished, we walked around for a few minutes, and she introduced me to some people she knew. We were standing there chatting when it suddenly hit me...

I have to leave. NOW. Something is very wrong.

Maybe you're hungry, eat a snack.

I sat in my car, ate a Larabar, and sipped water. I felt fatigued, nauseated, and disoriented. I realized I still had a thirty-minute drive home.

Can I drive myself? Should I call David?

Relax. Just focus on the drive, and if you feel it's necessary, pull over on the way home and call him.

I was on high alert while driving, and traffic was light since it was still early. As soon as I got home, I told David that I didn't feel well and was going to take a shower.

Yes, that's it. A shower always helps.

Typically, I love warm showers, but that day called for a cool shower. I got out and put on some clean clothes, then realized I couldn't keep my eyes open, so I laid down for a nap. When I woke up over an hour later, I felt *worse*. The nausea and fatigue were still strong, and I was freezing. I wrapped myself in a blanket and curled up on the couch, breaking into a cold sweat.

"Are you okay?" David asked.

"I'm freezing, tired, nauseous, and sweating."

"You might have a fever."

He was correct, I had a fever of 101.5. My body temperature typically hangs out in the mid 97's, so this was definitely a spike.

Well, that would explain why you felt so off during the race.

It was the Summer of 2022, and our family hadn't had Covid yet, but we kept the tests handy in case we needed them. My Covid test came back positive.

"I just ran a 4-mile race with Covid," I said to him, in complete shock.

I spent the rest of the day curled up in a blanket on the couch, with fatigue at a level I didn't remember *ever* experiencing. I didn't have any sinus issues, just the earth-shattering fatigue. I felt like I could barely move, and the next few days looked like this, laid up on the couch. This was not normal when I get sick, since I started eating so healthily a few years ago.

Exercise had become my crazy medicine, so taking that away weighed on me more than I anticipated. I sank into a slight depression because I felt like I could barely do anything physically and was stressing out about training for the upcoming triathlon.

I started walking outside...*slowly*. At first, I could only walk a total of a ½ mile. So, I walked that ½ mile at a time once a day, then twice a day, then three times a day until my body was able to handle walking a little bit farther each time. It took baby steps to get back to where I was, but those baby steps got me closer to my goal and feeling better than I would not moving at all.

One day while I was out on my geriatric walk, my dad drove by on his way out to have breakfast with his buddies. He slowed down, rolled down the window, and teased, "You sure are walking slow, you look like an 85-year-old woman out here!" I stuck my tongue out at him and continued to shuffle along at a snail's pace.

Like Robbie, my dad also seems to be allergic to exercise. He likes doing projects outside and shows up to our house on his riding lawnmower to cut our grass since they moved here from the beach, but he is not a fan of anything *labeled* exercise. However, if he could get paid for channel surfing, he would be a gazillionaire.

"I don't have time to be this exhausted, I have to train for the triathlon next month!" I whined to David.

Don't forget, your body is handling this significantly better than so many other people who have had Covid.

I hung my head, feeling sadness and deep empathy for those who had not been so fortunate. It was humbling and made me incredibly thankful to experience it. So, I continued to ease back into training. It took a full two weeks before I could even attempt jogging again, which only gave me four weeks to train.

This is your first triathlon, don't put too much pressure on yourself. Crossing that finish line is your only goal.

I listened to my body and did everything I could to prepare for the race. I swam in the pool twice a week, rode my bike twice a week, and ran 3-4 times a week. Some days the workouts would overlap, and I also did some brick workouts (bike and run back-to-back) so my body could handle going from a bike ride directly into a run. I also did a trial triathlon, where I wore my tri-suit and completed a shorter swim, bike, and run all at once. It wasn't the full distance of the race I was training for, but it was a practice round of what was to come.

All I need now is a new bike.

If my shirt were accurate, calorie consumption would be unlimited.

-8-

A NEW BIKE

"Why don't you get a cheap bike instead of going to the bike store? You know they'll be more expensive," David asked after I found a local bike shop that I was going to check out.

"I'm not getting a crappy bike for a *triathlon!*"

"They will be overpriced," said Mr. Logical.

"I'm just going to *look* at what they have."

"Yeah, right. I know you better than that."

I smirked. *He does know me better than that.*

On my way there, I thought about picking out a new bike and remembered when I first learned how to ride one when I was six years old. It was a huge deal to go from having a purple Cabbage Patch Kids Bigwheel to a pink Huffy bike with a long seat. My mom also found a cute basket for the front. My dad put training wheels on it to get me started, but my oldest brother insisted that after only a couple of weeks, I was ready to go without those training wheels.

"I'm scared!" I cried.

"I'm holding on to the back!" Michael replied.

I relaxed and started pedaling down the driveway while he held on to the back to keep me from falling over. Although a little unsteady, I did it with my big brother's help and guidance. I looked back and yelled, "I'm doing it!" expecting to see him right there.

Only Michael wasn't there, holding onto the bike. He had let go about ten seconds before I turned around, and smiled at me, riding alone. I panicked when I saw he wasn't holding on, lost my balance, and crashed down on the edge of the driveway, scraping up my knee and elbow in the process. I started crying.

"Why did you let go?? I CRASHED!!"

"I let go because I *knew* you could do it by yourself! And you did! You only crashed because you got scared that I wasn't there helping you, which means you *can* do it! See?"

"Oh," I sniffed and realized he was right.

A smile spread across my face, and he helped me pick up my wrecked bicycle off the driveway to try it again. I had the courage to do it this time without him holding on. He stood there with me as I took off from the start, but I made it out of the driveway and rode around in big circles throughout our cul-de-sac. I was thrilled to do it by myself and instantly became hooked.

He stood in the driveway as I circled, and yelled, "See? I *told* you! You're a professional now!"

Leave it to a 15-year-old big brother to slap you with an encouraging reality check. That wouldn't be the last time he challenged me to step outside my comfort zone.

I'd grown up riding simple bikes and had no idea they came in all different styles. Some bikes can even be as expensive as cars! When I walked into Outspokin' Bicycles in Irmo, my eyes widened as I looked around the collection of gorgeous bikes. In the center of the shop, the road bikes had aerodynamic lightweight frames and narrow tires. They were specially designed for speed and precision on paved surfaces. The customer service was fantastic, and they *almost* talked me into getting a road bike that was a perfect fit for my height. I imagined flying down the road like a lightning bolt, but the price tags veered me toward the mountain bikes. On the left side of the shop, the mountain bikes stood tall and sturdy with knobby tires ready for rough terrain. Their frames were built to endure the toughest challenges nature could throw at them. I pictured the dust clouds and adrenaline rush that came with tackling a trail sometime in the future. I fell in love with a bright red Trek Marlin 5, and it seemed like the ideal bike to start with.

A mountain bike was something I could use all the time, whether I was riding in my neighborhood, off-road, at a park, on trails, or going with my family on a leisurely ride. It was within my budget, so they ordered my size. And since I had a history of keeping bikes for many years, it was worth wiping out the spending money I had saved up for a rainy day. I picked out some accessories to go with it...including a new gel seat for my creampuff bottom. I'm not a fan of getting off a bike with sore giblets, so anything to reduce the discomfort until I could get used to it would be helpful.

The bike was ready a couple of weeks before the race. I grinned from ear to ear when I picked it up and brought it home to take it for a test ride. It was an absolute dream compared to that old hunk of junk.

This bike goes SO much faster!

The bike ride was the only portion of the race that I thought I could do well with. I felt ready for this race and couldn't wait for the big day to arrive.

Oldest Brother, Michael (left), Middle Brother, Robbie (middle), and little me.

-9-

OPENING THE FLOODGATES

"Have you trained for this more than my wife has?" Skibner's husband teased as we loaded her bike on the rack of my car.

"Yeah, I'm terrified of not being able to finish it, and I've been training regularly."

"Shut up, B! I don't care about *winning*; I'm doing this for *fun*!" she piped in.

"That's right!" I agreed.

He rolled his eyes at us and smiled. He had done several long-distance runs, including a marathon and multiple Spartan runs, so he wasn't impressed with our little sprint triathlon. Did we care? ABSOLUTELY NOT. We were doing this for *us*! For *fun*!

We hopped on the road to Mount Pleasant that afternoon but didn't get to the race site in time to pick up our packets. This was not surprising, considering traffic headed to Charleston on I-26 is almost always a hot mess. It wasn't a big issue, we just had to get there early the next morning to pick them up. We packed meals to eat in our hotel room to save money, so we went straight there to get settled in. I brought my grocery-store vegetable sushi rolls, happily indulged right after we got into our room, and were in our jammies by 7:00 pm. Being friends since fifth grade, we were like two little old ladies traveling together.

"Set the alarm for 5:30 am?" she asked at 9:30 while we were getting ready for bed.

"Let's do 5:00, just in case."

"Okay."

Little did I know how much I would regret this decision to lose an extra thirty minutes of sleep.

I slept horribly. Since we were in a hotel, I was woken up around 11:00 pm by people in the next room singing Happy Birthday. Normally I would have chimed in to sing along with them, but I desperately needed sleep and wasn't feeling the birthday vibe. I dozed off and woke up again at 1:45 am from hearing *more* noises. This time, I was awake until 4:00 before I finally fell back asleep. When the alarm went off an hour later at 5:00; I thought a bomb was exploding and the world was coming to an end. I wanted to go back to sleep so badly, but the fear of being late for the race was motivation enough to make myself get up.

I ate an apple, Banana Oatmeal Bar, mixed a packet of LMNT electrolytes in a bottle of water, and drank another bottle of water. My bowels emptied themselves early due to the nervousness of the race, so I felt five pounds lighter. We got ready, loaded our bikes up on the rack of the car, and headed to the race site. While loading our bikes, I noticed how much lighter her road bike was compared to my massive mountain bike and questioned how fast I would be able to go.

We picked up our race packets, got our numbers, and set up in the transition area. I looked around and saw an ocean of road bikes, desperately looking to see if there were any other mountain bikes like mine. I didn't see any and further doubted my decision to pass on getting a road bike, but I couldn't change the past.

I was in awe of the atmosphere. Although I had been to a few road races before, this was so much different. In the transition area, there were rows of road bikes hanging by their seats on a pole. Right under each bike was the racer's station with shoes, helmets, towels, and water bottles precisely placed to ensure a smooth transition from one leg of the race to the next.

We headed for the port-o-potties to empty our bladders, and we talked to a couple of ladies participating in the Duathlon part of the race. This option intrigued me as a run-bike-run, so I collected the idea in the back of my mind for the future. As we walked into the pool area, each section was marked according to our pace. The fastest pace was labeled, "I swam in college and am very fast."

I laughed out loud and cried, "Nope!"

We walked past it and headed farther to the back of the line labeled, "I like to hang back." *Perfect.* I had never swum 250 meters nonstop before that day and was more nervous about the swim than anything else. Thankfully, the pool was relatively shallow (even though it was *huge*) so if I needed to stop at any time, it shouldn't be a problem. The way the lanes were set up, we had to snake up and down each lane for the full 250 meters. A DJ was playing some upbeat music, so I was dancing in line to get my body warmed up. The atmosphere was charged with supportive energy as women of all ages, abilities, and backgrounds gathered at the start line to wait. We were all united by a shared goal and oozing with excitement and support.

I had three goals for the triathlon:
1. Don't drown in the pool
2. Jog the entire 2.5 miles without slowing down
3. Cross the finish line with a smile on my face

THE SWIM (250 meters)

The race started, and the ladies began getting into the pool. There were 85 people in this race, so we stood in line for what felt like an eternity while my anxiousness and excitement grew. They let us in one person at a time, waiting for the one ahead to get about halfway down the lane before letting the next person go. The fastest swimmers were in front, and I watched in awe as they swam like sailfish gliding through the water with speed and ease; making it look abnormally simple.

Is it as easy as they make it look?

I would soon prove that theory wrong.

I was extremely nervous about this part of the race since I had the least amount of training with it, so I was happy that it was the first portion to get it knocked out and move past it. Skibner was in front of me, and we made it into the water. The pool was quite choppy since there were so many people swimming their laps, so when I got in and started swimming, I was immediately hit with some unexpected issues.

First, water got into my right eye goggle. I put my contacts in for the race, so I could feel the water swishing around in my eye. I panicked.

Oh no, what if my contact comes out and I can't see during the rest of the race??

It's okay, you can be One-Eyed-Willie. Don't lose focus and keep moving forward.

I closed my right eye and kept swimming until I got to the wall to turn around. I flipped my goggles up quickly to let the water out, then put them back over my eyes and pushed off the wall. Not only did water get in my goggles *again*, but the pool was so choppy that every time I came up for air, I choked down water.

All the swim training I had done in the pool had been in very calm water since it was just me, and it was more like intervals because I took breaks. I wasn't used to being in an oversized pool with 85 other people swimming their little hearts out, creating constant waves that came crashing into my mouth and down my windpipe. As I approached the end of the next lap, there was a photographer taking pictures of each person as they approached.

Oh great, I'll look like a panicked housecat trying to claw its way out of the water.

Forget the photographer, who cares how you look? Just keep going, you have got to get through this. It's the hardest part of the race for you. Let's GO!!

I got a little more accustomed to the waves in the pool, but my freestyle was getting tired and the lady behind me was closing in quickly like she was going to pass me.

NO! She is not going to pass you! GO!!!

I switched up my stroke to somewhat of a lazy man's doggy paddle/breaststroke. I don't know exactly what it was, but I was moving forward, and that was all that mattered.

If you stop, it'll just slow down the progress of finishing this swim. GO!!!

The pool was big, but also shallow throughout *most* of it. In the middle of the laps, I was in the very center of the pool. When I got to this halfway point, I came up for a breath of air and choked down a big gulp of water. The lady behind me wasn't gaining on me, so I had a few extra seconds to spare. I needed to stop for a second to cough some of the water up, so I put my feet down to stand...but it was too deep for me to touch, and I felt myself flailing for a split second and panic started to develop again.

Keep going! Get to the wall so you can stop and get yourself together! You can do this!

I coughed, took a breath and moved forward, got to the wall, and stopped to cough up *all* of the water. Then, I pushed off the wall with massive force and plunged forward. The next couple of laps were steady and uneventful, just me coaching myself in my head.

You're almost there. KEEP GOING!!!

The last lap was like euphoria. Even though it was bright outside and there was no tunnel anywhere to be seen, this felt like a light at the end of the tunnel. I made it through the hardest part and was ecstatic to have finished the entire swim without drowning. The volunteers were at the edge of the pool, cheering. I climbed out of the pool and did what looked like a drunken jog over to the transition area.

Wow, I'm SO glad that part is done. I need to do more swim training.

I'm not a big fan of putting on shoes and socks while my feet are wet, but in these races, you suck it up and do what you have to. I sat down on the grass and dried off the lower parts of my legs and feet as much as possible before putting on my socks and shoes in a hurry. I took a swig of the electrolyte drink in my bag, put on my helmet and sunglasses, and then pulled my big ole' bulky mountain bike off the rack.

THE BIKE (8 miles)

When you participate in a triathlon, there are rules concerning the bike and when to mount and dismount. There are signs everywhere and you're given instructions, but when you're in the moment you must pay attention to what you're doing. I was jogging alongside my bike until I could hop on, with people telling me which way to go. Well, I was distracted because I took a right where I was supposed to take a left, and they called out to me in a panic. I turned around quickly and had to toss away that feeling of embarrassment to keep pedaling.

"Oh, you meant my *OTHER* left!!" I cried out and laughed at myself.

I still didn't see any other mountain bikes, and I figured my so-called logic of bringing mine to a triathlon race was extremely incorrect. Even though the new bike was significantly faster than the old one, it was like trying to win a race while riding on an elephant instead of a cheetah.

Skibner and I had finished the swim around the same time, and I was right behind her after my wrong-direction fiasco. I got a little overconfident and thought I was going to be Speedy Gonzales on the new bike. I passed her and a couple of other ladies, but shortly after that they all passed me, and I didn't catch up to them again on the ride.

I realized there was nothing I could do about the bike situation, so I enjoyed the ride and kept a steady pace for the full 8 miles. Hamlin Plantation was gorgeous with pristine landscaping, sidewalks throughout, and the homes were all Coastal-style and breathtaking. A lot of people who lived in the neighborhood were outside cheering for us along the route. About halfway through, there was a big family outside their house cheering and clapping. I was pretty much on a solitary ride, and they cheered for me as I rode by. The energy was infectious. We had to do two 4-mile loops in the neighborhood, but the bike route seemed to go by somewhat quickly...even though it was the most time-consuming part. I felt like a kid again, but this time I was in a race.

As I was finishing my last lap and heading to the transition area, one of the ladies in charge called out, "Go to the guy in the pink shirt!"

Every single volunteer was wearing a pink shirt. There were literally pink shirts EVERYWHERE.

"I don't see anyone wearing a pink shirt!"

She didn't appreciate my joke, but the other pink-shirted people laughed.

"Over here!" one guy shouted and pointed me to the transition area. I dismounted and jogged alongside my bike to put it on the rack, took a swig of electrolytes, tore off my helmet, and wobbled out for the run.

THE RUN (2.5 miles)

If you have never tried to run immediately after riding a bike, it's... *interesting*. The first time I attempted this, I felt like my legs were noodles that had just come out of a freshly boiling pot of water. Thankfully, the first time I tried that was about three weeks before this race, so I took the time to get enough practice doing a run after a bike ride.

I started a slow and steady jog out of the transition area, trying to make sure I followed the correct directions this time, so I didn't make a fool out of myself by going the wrong way again. After getting on the course, the self-coaching in my head started up, this time in full force. The run was when I needed it the most.

All you have to do is run 2 ½ miles.

I was jogging by myself again, seeing a few ladies sprinkled both in front of and behind me. Not even half a mile into the run, I started to get stitches in both of my sides.

What in the world? Ugh...NO! Not now!
Just keep it steady and don't stop!

I continued to keep my pace, but I was getting tired. I had noticed during my training sessions that I got stronger, faster, and more energized during the second half of my runs...but that was only if I started out at an easy, steady pace. Coming off hot and sprinting will wear you out fast, and these races are all about being consistent, so you don't burn out. The saying, "Slow and steady wins the race," helped me through these events when I talked to myself; and I talked to myself a lot.

There was one water station set up on the run, but we passed it twice since it was an out-and-back route. The first time through, I didn't feel like I needed it. I was still trying to get used to eating and drinking while moving during these races, so I knew it would take some practice. However, it's crucial for hydrating and fueling because you do *not* want to run out of gas in the middle of a race. Endurance events are a test of how strong your mind is to push your way through when you think you can't keep going. This is a mindset I did not possess during the first part of my life, but I refused to let it reflect what the remaining years would look like. I'm not going to waste the next 40ish years with that negativity in my mind and heart.

I thought I had gone farther when I saw the 1-mile sign, and a wave of shock ran through me.

Is that for real? Seriously?? I've only gone ONE mile? That can't be right. Dangit!

Focus on moving forward!

The ladies in this race ranged in age from 10-79. During the run, I passed the 79-year-old woman and was eager to see her. I hoped to be like her when I grow up, still out doing these events in thirty years.

"I'm going to tell my mom about you! You're amazing!!" I exclaimed.

She laughed and said, "You tell her to get out here next year, if I can do this she can too!"

As I kept running, I caught up to Skibner, who had slowed down since the run was her least favorite part. She'd blown past me earlier on her nimble road bike, leaving me in her dust. Our playful banter is always a highlight, and the woman walking with her probably thought I was just some random nutjob approaching from behind. We cheered each other on as I passed, and I reminded her with a grin that mimosas were waiting for us at the finish line.

"LET'S GO! WE'VE GOT THIS!!!"

Although I was cheering for her, I was completely exhausted and struggling immensely.

SUCK IT UP, BUTTERCUP!! You can do this! Don't slow down now!!

Self-coaching works wonders, especially since I was running by myself most of the way. The volunteers and spectators were incredibly supportive and constantly called out, "Great job! Keep going! You're doing awesome!" Which was so helpful and motivating. I love and appreciate the volunteers at *all* events.

The last half mile was tough, but again I saw the light at the end of the tunnel. If you've ever participated in any kind of race event, there's a line of people coming up to the finish line, cheering. It's extremely motivating, and we all need that when hanging on by a thread...which I was physically at this point, but mentally I wanted to sprint another full mile. My body wasn't up for that. As I came through the clearing and saw how close the finish line was, a smile spread across my face. I didn't sprint, but I picked up my pace because it was so close I could feel it, see it, and hear it.

You're almost there! Let's GO!!!!!!

I propelled through the last stretch on the tree-shaded path, ran under the finish line with a HUGE smile, and threw my hands in the air.

YOU DID IT!!! YOU FINISHED!!! YOU JUST COMPLETED A TRIATHLON!!!!

I heard the announcer call out, "Here is number 17, Erin Courtney!" and I blushed.

A few volunteers were waiting for me with my finisher's gift, which was a necklace engraved with, "Do the hard things." I walked over to the transition area to grab a Liquid IV packet and poured it into an ice-cold bottle of water. I quickly walked over to the finish line to wait for Skibner to come through. She came through with a big smile on her face as well, and we hugged. A few minutes later, we were walking around in the sun, and I was sipping on my electrolytes when it hit me; dizziness, fatigue, and slight nausea.

Sit down in the shade and eat something.

I found a cooler spot in the shade close to the finish line and pulled out an RX Bar to nibble on while I rested. At first, I was worried that I overdid it, or something was wrong, but felt better after eating and finished drinking my electrolytes. I sat there for about ten minutes to recuperate before getting back up and heading to the front to cheer for the last participants to cross the finish line and wait for the awards ceremony.

We all gathered around as the top 3 winners were announced overall and in each age group (one of my favorite parts of any race). The community, energy, and support at this event were amazing. I'm competitive by nature, so when the ladies in my age group took the podium, I daydreamed about one day being able to stand up there.

Maybe you'll get there one day...but it takes time, consistency, and dedication. You must start somewhere. Be patient, Baby Yoda.

All three goals were accomplished, and I was beside myself. The realization hit me after the race...

*Now I need a **road** bike.*

This is my "panicked housecat" stroke. David teases me that I look like a bug wearing the goggles, which is clearly a sign of true love.

Crossing the finish line with a smile on my face and hands in the air.

-10-

PROGRESS OVER PERFECTION

I signed up for the Labor Day 5k a couple of months in advance, while David waited until the week before to register. Although he'd been training on his treadmill before work, he didn't want to commit early to participate in the event. Why? I have no idea what goes on in that brain of his, and it's probably best that way.

The day before the race, I went out for a lake day with my family. The kids went on the tube, and halfway through the day, we ended up pulling the tube into the back of the boat to ride around. While I was helping Michael pull the massive tube out of the water, my left foot stepped back and the arch came down *very* hard on a solid plastic doorstop that keeps the back door of the boat open. I winced and cried out in pain from how sharp it went into my foot. I hobbled over to take a seat and examined the damage. At first, it was okay, but it progressively got worse. Ten minutes later, it was swollen, tender, and turned dark purple. I took an ice pack out of my lunchbox, held it against my boo-boo for about 5 minutes, and kept it propped up.

You have got to be kidding me. Not before the race tomorrow!!!

Worst case scenario, take some ibuprofen and suck it up. You don't have to skip tomorrow unless it's absolutely necessary.

I limped on it the rest of the day, took some ibuprofen before bed, crossed my fingers and toes, and hoped for the best.

I started to think I had pre-race anxiety, based on my sleep the night before races. The kids spent the night with my parents since we needed to leave the house by 6:30 am, allowing them to sleep in and hang out with Grammy and Grampy. I woke up at 1:30, 3:30, then up at 5:00.

WHY AM I AWAKE???

David had the alarm set for 5:50 to make sure we had time to get up since he likes to drink coffee. At the time, I preferred to save coffee for after we got back home since I was already having pre-race jitters and didn't want to make it worse with caffeine. I drank two full glasses of water to make sure I had plenty of hydration and packed a water bottle with my LMNT electrolytes to sip on half of it before the race. I debated eating before we ran since it was so early in the morning and decided to fast for this one since it was short. David got up when his alarm went off and we got ready, then headed out to the car right before 6:30. We pulled out of the driveway, and I checked my email for any information I may have missed.

"The race doesn't start until 8:30!!!" I cried after we pulled out of the neighborhood.

"What?? Do I need to turn around?"

"Yeah, let's turn around. There's no reason to get there over an hour early if we don't have to, and I'll go ahead and eat something."

He's not a morning person and complained about us having to get up so early. He drank another cup of coffee and ate his Pumpkin Cinnamon Roll Muffin, so I had an apple and Banana Oatmeal Bar. I wanted to eat something light that would be enough to give me energy for the race without weighing me down. I bugged him to drink some Gatorade before the race so he could avoid dehydration, so he sipped it at home and in the car. We both have learned how crucial it is to stay hydrated, especially in the heat. Let's face it, we're not getting any younger and this southern heat can be brutal during the summer. Forty-five minutes went by, and we were on the road...*again*. He reached over and grabbed my hand during the car ride. By now, he had time to wake up and transition into his human form.

"I like doing these races together," he smiled.

"Me too!"

He's much faster than me, being a natural endurance athlete with his tall, slender frame, and has been running on and off for years. Running comes naturally to him, but it took much more time and effort for me before I experienced the enjoyment of it. I had to work hard before the benefits started to pay off.

"Thank you for supporting me during all this, I know it's a big shift since I started running," I said.

"You don't have to thank me for supporting you."

"Yes, I do. I was reading about runners who don't have the support and stop running because they're not embraced by people who believe in them. They give up too soon because of surrounding negativity and miss out on the opportunity."

"Really?"

"You're the only one in the family who truly supports me doing this. They think I'm crazy and don't understand why I'm doing it," I said, staring out the window.

"Let's be honest, you *are* crazy, but not when it comes to this. I think it's great that you found something you enjoy."

"Hey, my crazy comes naturally, and you *chose* to marry me. So that means you're crazy by choice."

"We're crazy together," he said as he squeezed my hand.

This shift had not been easy, but it had become much more rewarding than I ever thought it would be. Crossing the finish line-ANY finish line- was still surreal...but it was worth the effort. Just then, it hit me that I hadn't thought to check on my foot from the boat day fiasco, which meant there was no pain.

"Well, it didn't hurt this morning, so I didn't even think to check on it. That's a good thing!" I smiled.

We arrived at the race site and immediately found the port-o-potties. His coffee and my water went right through us. Skibner was there to run as well, so we walked to the start line together. We're all at different paces, so we split up during the route but reconnected at the finish line. Endurance events are fascinating. One minute I'm passing people who are younger, fitter, and stronger than me. The next minute, I'm getting passed by moms pushing strollers and people old enough to have adult grandchildren. I had learned over the past five months of training that being steady and consistent is crucial; like everything else in life.

While on the route, I spotted a mom pushing a stroller. At first, her little 2-year-old was jogging beside her as I passed them, and it was adorable. A few minutes later, the little girl was inside the stroller, and they passed me.

I called out to her, "You are my hero!"

She laughed, and we ran at a steady pace together for about 5 minutes, chatting along the way. She was in her late twenties and said she ran cross-country in high school. I tend to strike up short conversations with strangers before, during, and after races.

Forget that she's pushing a stroller...she's 15 years younger than you, ran cross-country in high school, and you're running alongside her! That is progress!

While approaching a hill, a volunteer was standing on the side of the road cheering for us. I called out to him, "You're cheering, but not mentioning anything about that hill up ahead!"

"You can do it! Just keep going, it'll go downhill after that!"

As I worked my way up the hill, I realized it was worse than expected and I wasn't prepared for it.

You should do some hill training.

Even my inner voice was struggling on the hill. I rounded the corner that started the decline and saw the finish line ahead, with a huge line of people on both sides cheering for everyone who came through. The mom who I was talking to had gotten ahead of me, and I couldn't blame her if she wasn't going to let some 42-year-old rookie beat her in a race.

You get it, girl.

I looked for David and spotted him smiling, clapping, and cheering when he saw me. This is when the surge of energy exploded, and I picked up the pace.

I was running through the lines of people by myself, and several people held out their hands for a high five. I reached out and slapped several hands as I went by, and they cheered even louder. A photographer was at the finish line, snapping pictures of each finisher. You would have thought I won the whole race by the smile on my face and throwing my hands up in the air, but I didn't care. I knew I had finished feeling better than ever and had made so much progress from when I started. All I wanted to do that day was beat my best average pace per mile, which was 11:48. When the race results were posted, I about fell over. I knew I had bettered my average pace, but I was NOT expecting a 45-second pace per mile improvement!! I was ecstatic!

This is why you're doing this, right here. The thrill of finishing the race, the feeling of seeing progress and accomplishment being a middle-aged mom doing something she never thought she could do.

This was why I kept going. This was why I had no intention of stopping. This was why I wanted to continue to do this for as long as I possibly could. This was why I was getting more and more comfortable with stepping outside my comfort zone and challenging myself to try something I never thought was possible, whether it's big or small. Every little bit counts, and it all started with running.

Running is just the tip of the iceberg.

-11-

A WOMAN'S CURSE

David used to tease me about running the same 1.6-mile loop in our neighborhood. When I run outside, I repeat the same loop based on the distance I'm running, whether it's 3 miles or 10 miles.

"I would get *so* bored running the same loop repeatedly," he said.

"I love it! I know the distance and route, and if I need to use the bathroom, I can stop at our house or my parents to do that before getting right back out there. If there's an emergency, you're close by and I have a bunch of our neighbors' phone numbers as well. I just plug in my music and go. It's great!"

"Why don't you go across the highway and down that dirt road? It's a great place for a run."

The road he is referring to is over a mile long, very wooded, and has only a few houses spaced out on large lots. It's a beautiful, rural setting that I would happily run with another person anytime but avoid going by myself.

"I am not running down that road alone unless I'm going to disguise myself as a dude. I'll go by Aaron."

"You're silly. What does that have to do with it?" he laughed.

I sighed, "You're a guy. You don't get it."

"What do you mean?"

"All it takes is one wrong person to see me running down that road by myself and make a bad decision. There are no neighbors, no cameras, just woods. I'm not comfortable running there alone."

"Yeah, but you run during the day when it's light outside, *and* you're a black belt."

"It doesn't matter," I said sadly. "You have *no* idea how many women are attacked in broad daylight. There are many situations where I must be careful that you don't have to worry about, simply because you're a man. I stick to the neighborhood and treadmill while running alone, and I'm happy with that."

One day while scrolling through social media, I came across a story in the news about a mom in her thirties who disappeared one morning after she went for a run. A short while later, the news popped up that her body was found. She was a teacher who left behind two young children and her husband. My heart was broken for her and her family. All I could think about was what she went through before losing her life, and how terrifying it must have been.

She *shouldn't* have to be extra careful while going out for a run. She *shouldn't* have to look out for danger. She *shouldn't* have to run in daylight to decrease her risk of getting attacked. She *shouldn't* have to run with someone else; she *should* be able to run when she wants and where she wants without any fear of jeopardizing her safety in the process.

Unfortunately, this is the society we live in. I can only hope the culture will change, but it will take a long time to get there. It reminded me of a time that I will never forget...

In college, I lived with my two best friends in a huge neighborhood on the old Air Force Base in Myrtle Beach. It was all townhome-style rental units, with sidewalks throughout. Most mornings before going to school, I would do a workout video followed by a 2-mile walk in the neighborhood. It was always the time of morning when it was bright, and the streets were busy with people outside. The neighborhood had a few sketchy areas, and I avoided certain streets simply because it didn't feel right. But overall, I felt safe on these walks during the day and took them regularly.

One morning, I had to get up extra early for school and went through my routine of a workout video followed by a 2-mile walk. I put my shoes on, threw on a sweatshirt and headphones, and headed out the door. It was 5:00 am, cold, and still pitch-black outside. I walked out the front door and turned on the sidewalk.

Suddenly, I stopped dead in my tracks. The most overwhelming feeling of fear held me there, completely frozen. I looked ahead and felt something deep inside my gut radiate throughout my entire body.

Don't go.

I stood there for a few seconds, shook my head, and started moving forward.

No, I'm going.

I took a few more steps, then it felt like something grabbed me by the shoulders, held me like a statue, and *screamed* inside my head, far more intense than the first warning.

DO...NOT...GO!!!!!

I looked around and saw no one, standing there for a few more seconds. I had never felt anything so intense in my life. It shook me to my core, I felt it in every inch of my body, and I couldn't move. I was paralyzed.

I am strong-willed and can be incredibly stubborn, and if I have my mind set on something, I will do it. But something felt utterly wrong at this moment. As much as I didn't want to go back inside, I turned around and headed back through the front door, locking it behind me. I sat down on the couch, the feeling of fear instantly released, and I felt safe.

What was that?!?!

I was in a deep state of confusion, wondering what just happened. I had never experienced anything so overwhelmingly intense.

What kept me from going?

My roommate and bestie, Amy, walked in the living room and saw me sitting on the couch with a perplexed look on my face and asked if I was okay, so I explained to her what happened.

"Oh my gosh. Well, I'm glad you didn't go!"

"I still don't understand what just happened but feel it was the right decision to come back inside."

A few years later, I read a statistic about how women are more often targeted in the dark, early hours of the morning. The hairs stood up on my arms as I immediately thought back to this moment. Over the next few years, I learned even more about safety while training in martial arts...specifically for women. I have a running book with an entire section on safety for women. Don't run by yourself in the dark, don't wear headphones, don't run in secluded areas, carry mase with you, etc. It *shouldn't* be this way. To say that the safety precautions women need to take more than men is extremely unfortunate, but it is what it is. We have no control over what other people do in any circumstance, only the decisions we make for ourselves.

Maybe it's my anxiety, OCD, or the feeling I experienced in college...but either way, I choose to be overly cautious when it comes to running alone, avoiding dark parking lots, and the countless other circumstances that women have to consider. Despite these precautions, the underlying need for such measures highlights the ongoing challenge of ensuring that women can exercise freely and safely without fear.

Does this mean I am exempt from something bad happening? Of course, not...but it does increase safety and decrease the risks. As time goes on, I'll become more comfortable and assess what feels safe and what doesn't, depending on the situation.

This "curse" of precaution often feels unfair and exhausting. It's a reminder that while many navigate the world with a sense of freedom, women are taught from a young age that the responsibility to protect themselves lies heavily on their shoulders. The mental and emotional toll of these constant precautions can be draining. In a world where this sense of hyper-awareness is normalized for women, the underlying question remains: Why should the burden of safety be a woman's curse rather than society's responsibility?

I fear we'll never know, but in the meantime, I will listen to my intuition when it's screaming at me and take precautions when necessary.

-12-

YODA DEFEATS HITLER

One of the many things I had learned was that endurance training requires a strong, positive mindset. A negative mindset will keep you from accomplishing your goals, while a positive mindset will keep you going to the finish line. It blew my mind how much of a shift my inner voice made in just a few months and had become such an important part of my life. Before, it was like I had both Yoda and Hitler in my head, and Hitler was running the show with abusive negativity.

The new inner voice is Yoda who kicked Hitler to the curb. I'm pretty sure it throat-punched it, too. It's strong, energetic, positive, encouraging, and it's not making any excuses for what I *can't* do; only focusing on what I *can* do. It helps me move forward instead of focusing on the past. It gives me grace when needed, but also pushes and challenges me to not give up. It lovingly reminds me when I need to put on my Big Girl Panties. It's what I never knew I truly needed.

I couldn't escape it, and I didn't want to. It became the positive voice I had given others but been unable to give myself...until it changed. It is the voice I wish I had for so many years. Although I can't change the past, I appreciate the shift because I will never forget what it felt like living in the dark both mentally and emotionally. It's not a place I ever want to go back to.

Before my second She-Tris Triathlon at Carnes Crossroads in Summerville, I made a brash decision by purchasing a road bike. Remember the one that wasn't in my budget when I bought the mountain bike? Yep, that's the one. It was an emotional choice, but I broke down and put it on a credit card. It wasn't my finest decision-making moment, but I planned on keeping the bike for a long time, putting many miles on it. That was my justification, and I stuck to it.

The day before the race, I felt incredibly run down and took a nap in the middle of the day, which is very rare for me. That afternoon, I spiked a low-grade fever, and my heart sank as the thoughts of the summer flooded my mind. As I sat on the edge of the bed and contemplated if racing this event was a good idea, the thought of running the 4-mile race with Covid in July went through my mind, David walked in and saw the look on my face.

"What's wrong?"

"I'm not sure if I should do the race," I said with my head down. We still planned on going for a weekend family trip, but I was scared to put my body through something it might not be able to handle.

"I think you should still plan on doing it because you'll regret it if you don't. If you feel worse in the morning, just make a decision then."

Reason #1,364 why I married this man.

We packed up the car and hit the road. We got caught in traffic and didn't make it in time to pick up my race packet (*again*), which meant we'd have to get up earlier than planned. For dinner, I loaded up on a salad bowl with greens, brown rice, black beans, pinto beans, corn salsa, and guacamole at Chipotle and felt *much* better. We settled in at the hotel and went to bed early in hopes of a good night's sleep.

RACE DAY

Except for Alex, the rest of us slept horribly. I slept 4 solid hours, but surprisingly felt decent when I woke up. None of us wanted to be up this early and out the door, so we were dragging as we got up and dressed. I ate a Banana Oatmeal Bar and an apple, along with electrolytes and an extra bottle of water. I looked at the current temp outside, and it said 52 degrees.

FIFTY. TWO. DEGREES.

I immediately stressed out over jumping in the pool wearing my little Tri suit in chilly weather. We arrived about 15 minutes later than we should have, and I ran around in a panic. I was one of the later arrivals, trying to get my race packet with my bib and chip timer strapped to my ankle and having them write my race number on my shoulders and age on my calf.

Just as everything started, I found my place in line waiting for the swim, and I stood there shivering. There was so much energy around me, and I was surrounded by smaller groups of women who already knew each other. I typically enjoy meeting and talking to new people...but I was *cold*. As I stood there for about 15 minutes, I watched everyone around me, taking everything in and thinking about how miserable that swim would be.

Suck it up, Buttercup.

Like clockwork for these events, Yoda voice showed up ready to race and was already coaching me along. It wasn't going anywhere, and it wasn't going to let *me* go anywhere, either. It was ready to show me what I was capable of achieving.

Look at the steam coming up from the pool. That means the water is warmer than the air, so it will feel good getting in there to swim. You'll be fine. LET'S DO THIS!!

THE SWIM (250 meters)

The weather warmed up to a whopping 56 degrees by the time the race began, and we started hopping in the pool one by one. I had been shivering in my suit for almost an hour before getting in the water.

Like the first race, I chose a spot farther back in the line for the swim. I wasn't a terrible swimmer, but I wasn't fast. I started chatting with some ladies in line while waiting to start. I was not the only one who was freezing my booty off, and it turns out several of these ladies were just as nervous about the swim as I was at my first event. I thought about how Alex was probably harassing David that he was bored, cold, wanted to go to the playground, etc. but I looked over and saw they were still off to the side of the fence, watching me.

When I jumped into the pool, I was delighted to feel the warmth of the water. I was more prepared for this swim than the last race and had a good start while keeping a steady pace. We snaked up and down the lanes of the pool like last time, passing people on the other side of our lane. About halfway through, I passed another lady who was going a little slower. When you pass someone, the etiquette is to tap them on the foot to let them know you're passing.

Just keep going steady, don't stop!! You're already halfway through!

Another lane over, I kept plugging along and saw a woman headed toward me, doing a backstroke, and she couldn't see me. She must have been worn out because she was all over the place. I moved over to the far side of the lane to avoid bumping into each other, but she had also veered into my side as well. I pushed forward and sped up, going right along the edge of the rope for our lane...but didn't make it in time before we ended up colliding head-on.

"Oh my gosh, I'm so sorry!" she cried.

"That's okay, keep going!" I cheered back at her.

Like the last race, I was right in the center of the pool where it was a little too deep for me to touch after she and I collided. I tried to touch the bottom but couldn't reach it.

Don't panic, keep going!

I pulled it together with a burst of energy and surged forward. It's harder to stop when you're swimming than riding a bike or running. I rounded the last lane and hoped to put a little speed in, but I was already giving it all I had and was wearing out.

Good grief, swimming is the area I need the most work for my endurance.

Don't worry about going fast, just keep moving forward. You're almost there!

It's going to be freezing when I get out of here!

It'll keep you cool for the ride!

I made it to the steps and heard my family cheering from the fence. I was slightly disoriented but kept moving to make it to the transition area to get on my bike. Although it felt great in the warm water, it didn't take long for the shivers to come back with a vengeance as I got out of the pool, soaking wet in the chilly weather.

You'll warm up quickly!

THE BIKE (9 miles)

My bike transition took a little longer than I expected, trying to dry off while shivering from the swim. My bike and everything I needed were stuffed in with everyone else's items like a packed can of sardines. I was terrified that I left something out or would forget a necessity during transitions. It's a bit of a challenge trying to use your fine motor skills while freezing, so even putting on my shoes and socks over partially wet feet was more difficult than usual. I started to get frazzled.

Chill, girl. This transition is not going to make or break you. Just grab what you need to get on the bike.

I got my shoes and socks on, threw on my helmet and sunglasses, grabbed my bike, and headed out of the transition area. After passing the mount sign to hop on my bike, I jumped on and started pedaling. My family was there with their phones, taking videos and pictures, cheering loudly as I passed, and I smiled at them.

Having them here fills my soul.

My feet were cold, and the cool wind blowing on my wet tri-suit and skin registered, but it was time for adrenaline to take over.

Yeah baby, let's put this road bike to the test! Push those pedals and GO!!

I pushed to get some speed, following the turns of the course. This event took place in a large neighborhood like the last triathlon, and there were police officers and volunteers everywhere to guide us along the route. Since this was a different neighborhood and not in my town, I wasn't familiar with the route, so I kept my eyes peeled to avoid going in the wrong direction again.

It surprised me how much faster and smoother the ride was on the road bike compared to the mountain bike. It was *easy*...so I started going fast. In the last race, I didn't pass anybody. No seriously, I didn't pass *anybody*. As the route went on, we did three loops. I started passing a few people, and it fueled my adrenaline even more.

Alright, Speedy Gonzales. Don't get too excited and wear yourself out before the run.

After the first 3-mile loop, my quads were feeling the burn. I kept a steady pace and enjoyed the ride because it was still so exhilarating. Something about the wind blowing in my face and pedaling for a smooth ride is relaxing...well, other than the part that you're pushing yourself and your muscles until they're screaming at you for mercy.

No mercy, Buttercup! You've got this!

Every time I passed the main area with all the spectators, my family was there, cheering loudly for me.

"Yay, Mommy!!"

"Go Erin!!"

"Great job, Mom!!"

I couldn't help but smile every time I heard and saw them. By the third loop, I was familiar with the route. We still had to watch for cars since the roads weren't closed off, and I came up behind a car driving slowly on the last loop. There was an upcoming speed hump, so they slowed down even more to go over it. I wasn't about to slow down, so I came up on the right side and pushed as fast as I could to get around them. I was nervous they might not see me and veer to the right where I was, but I made it past and kept going.

You just passed a car! On your bicycle!

I chuckled to myself and finished up the last quarter mile of the loop, headed to the transition area to drop off my bike and start on the run.

Oh wow, I still have to run 3 miles...

Suck it up! You've got this!!

Okay, Yoda.

THE RUN (3 miles)

At first, I wasn't sure how the run would pan out, since I struggled on this final portion of the first triathlon. My main goal was to stay steady and run at a turtle's pace the entire route without slowing down to walk. I didn't have my watch to track mileage, pace, or heart rate, so I was winging it.

Just keep going, like a Ninja Turtle.

As I kept moving, the run got easier. Yes, *easier*. I was still cool on the bike but became comfortably warm on the run. The neighborhood had sidewalks and paved trails for the route, and I wish I could have gotten a picture of the two large ponds I circled in the neighborhood. When I came up to the first pond, I was the only person on the trail except a spectating couple on the other side. I spotted a warning sign for alligators, and my imagination spiraled immediately.

Oh, isn't that nice? Alligators in a pond and I'm out here by myself. Hopefully, they're not hungry and looking for breakfast.

Pfft. You're a Ninja Turtle, remember? It's probably a little gator that you could drop kick into next week. Just enjoy the scenery and keep your eyes peeled.

I relaxed and kept running. Suddenly, it hit me with amazement that this was the easiest run I had done so far.

You're all warmed up now and it's the last leg of the race, you've got this!!

Earlier when I was standing in the pool line talking to some of the other ladies, I noticed several of them had a strong running background before doing their first triathlon. Even though we were about the same pace in the swim, and I was ahead of them on the bike, they flew past me on the run. I cheered for them as they passed by and thought about how my running game needed more work.

You'll get there, it just takes time. You just started running 6 months ago, give yourself some grace! It's more about the journey and progress than anything else.

As I continued to run, I felt even better and felt a deep level of enjoyment circulate through my veins like never before.

How is this even possible?

Perseverance, baby. See how consistency and not giving up have paid off in the past few months? Just imagine what you're capable of achieving one, five, even ten years from now...

After mile 2, I started to get tired. Some of the volunteers were along the route guiding us and yelling, "You're almost there!" I smiled and threw my hands in the air as I ran by. After a few more twists and turns, I could hear it getting close.

There's the finish line! GO!!!!!

I picked up the pace significantly as I rounded the last corner. My family was in plain sight, and the kids started jumping up and down, screaming when they saw me. David's smile as he saw me coming up was heartwarming, I smiled and waved as I passed. The announcer called out my race number and name as I went under the finish line, and I was grinning from ear to ear.

Since I was competing against my previous times from the first triathlon, I DID IT!! My swim improved by 34 seconds, my bike pace improved by 37 seconds per mile, and my run pace improved by 11 seconds per mile! As expected, the road bike made a HUGE difference compared to the mountain bike. My family's support motivated me to push harder each time I passed by them. When I finished, the feeling was euphoric. I thought about how six months ago, I couldn't even run two blocks without stopping.

How did I get here?

You're here because you haven't given up! See what happens when you keep moving forward?

Crossing the finish line with David, Alex, and Kaitlyn in the background for support. This is the perfect example of a picture being worth a thousand words.

-13-

THE BET

Although I have received some good advice over the years from many people, there is one piece of advice that stood out, and I consistently remind myself of it regularly. Another mom I've had the privilege of knowing is the biggest ball of energy I have ever met. Stacey is a fitness instructor, personal trainer, and takes care of her family's gorgeous property in the country. We have had many conversations about inspiration because she is a *huge* inspiration to me. I told her I wanted to be like her when I grew up, and she laughed.

"I'll give you the basics I live by," she said.

1. Lead by example
2. Be a positive influence
3. Stay in your lane

I have carried this advice with me since then and apply it to every relationship possible, especially our kids. Honestly, the last part is the hardest for me, being strong and vocal. Throw in motherhood with that and it's even *more* challenging. I don't want to control what other people do, but I want to help them when I can. It sounds exhausting to try and manage what everyone else does with their lives. The best thing I can do for myself and everyone else around me is to follow her advice and try to be a light in the darkness, even if it's only a drop in the bucket. Every little bit helps.

My family is full of Carolina Gamecocks fans, and we like to get together to watch football games during the Fall. We're not die-hard fans whose day is ruined if we don't win and we do cheer for Clemson as long as we're not playing against them, but we enjoy watching the games. I think it's much more about the socialization of watching it with each other than the actual game itself. We sit around the TV, busting each other's chops between spurts of making sports commentary during the game, and of course, eating lots of food.

One day while we were together, the subject of running came up like it had been a lot over the past few months since I started. They all think I'm nuts. My oldest brother, Michael, thinks I will lose interest in running and move on to something else because it's a sport that takes a lot of time to build endurance and requires consistency. I have ADD and a history of losing interest before really putting in the time and long-term effort to see the benefits. It's been a lifelong struggle, and our whole family is notorious for it. He also points out that I'm getting older and won't be able to run like I could have twenty years ago. Although it's more challenging in my forties, it's not impossible with hard work. This is exactly why I have such a deep appreciation for David's support and common interest.

"I love seeing the progress of running faster because I never thought I could run distances in the first place," I told them.

"I think it's great that you're doing this, I just have never been able to run," Robbie said.

"The races are fun to watch, there's so much energy at them!" my mom piped in. She loves coming to the events to wait for us at the finish line and sometimes walks the 5k distance with Kaitlyn.

My dad said nothing, but I knew what was going through his overactive noggin. He was worried that anytime I go out for a run, I'll get hit by a car, snatched up by a stranger, or drop dead of a heart attack because he heard that happened to *one* runner 40 years ago. I reminded him that it's much better than sitting on the couch eating donuts, but to him, the best-case scenario is that I walk on the treadmill at home or don't tell him whenever I go out for a run. Bless his little overly paranoid heart.

"Don't forget that you're not getting any younger. You'll plateau soon and then it'll just go downhill from there," Michael said.

Although he knew my history, he didn't know about the mental shift I had made; how I saw things so differently and was no longer who I *used* to be. He didn't see the growth I had already experienced.

"Wanna bet on that?" I challenged him.

"Yes. I bet you won't be faster than you are right now in three years," he stated. He seemed confident with his prediction.

I laughed. "Three years? Seriously, you don't think I'll be faster in *three years*??"

"Like I said, you're not getting any younger, and you must be *consistent* to get faster."

There it is. He doesn't think I will stick with it.

"I'll take that bet. A hundred bucks say my 5k pace will be faster in three years than it is right now," I clarified as I pulled out my phone calendar to set a reminder for October 9th, 2025.

I would win the bet if I had a time of less than 34 minutes for a 5k. There's nothing like someone telling you that you can't do something that ignites a fire under your butt.

Watch me, bro.

This dude had NO idea what he was getting himself into by making a bet like this. He'd better start saving his pennies because I couldn't wait to collect my hundred bucks.

"He said *what??*" David was appalled when I got home and told him.

"Our family doesn't realize it, but we grew up with a fixed mindset. This is exactly what I want to change about myself moving forward and shifting into a *growth* mindset. The fixed mindset has only held me back, but I won't let it do that anymore."

"As I've said before, if you tell yourself that you can't do something without putting in the work and consistency, you're automatically setting yourself up for failure," he said.

He has had a growth mindset since I met him, and I wanted it too. However, changing your mindset is not an easy task and takes a lot of time, effort, and commitment. I had no idea that I grew up with a fixed mindset until I read a book about it, and it was like a lightning bolt hit me with a full force of realization. It quickly became a rollercoaster of emotions with a rapid replay of flashbacks throughout my life with how many times I had given up when I could have succeeded if I had just stuck with it...but I didn't know any better.

You don't know what you don't know. Learn from this and move forward.

It doesn't happen overnight, but it is worth it to lose the feeling of being hopeless and worthless. I'm very familiar with those feelings, but I refused to spend the rest of my years with that outlook. It was time for a change. It was *past* time for a change.

You'll be one hundred dollars richer in three years, to put towards your new collection of running shoes.

The yang to my yin; or is it yin to my yang?

-14-

HOMERUN RACE

While scrolling through race events for 2022, I came across the Ray Tanner 12k and 5k. Ray Tanner was the former head baseball coach at the University of South Carolina. As I read information about the race, I saw the options for the distances and decided to choose the longer option, the 12k (7.45 miles). David and I both signed up for it. Why? Well, other than being *crazy*, we were looking for a challenge and needed preparation for our first Half-Marathon coming up a month later.

The most exciting part of this race was that the finish line was crossing the home plate of the Gamecock Baseball Stadium!! Along with being a Gamecock fan, I grew up playing softball and was on my high school varsity team; so, this sparked my interest and excitement. We had attended UofSC baseball games from the spectator position. This time we would get to run onto the field and cross home plate!

"Yeah, I don't care about that," David laughed.

"Well, I *do*! That'll be awesome!" I cried. The banter between us keeps our marriage entertaining.

Two weeks before the race, I strained the tendon connecting my quad with tibialis which forced me to rest and recover, and I got worried.

If I can't train, how in the world will I be ready for a HALF-MARATHON next month?!?!

One week before the 12k, I knew that running the 7.5 miles with an injury wasn't my greatest idea ever. So, I found out I could easily drop down to the 5k option instead of doing the 12k. I was hesitant at first because I felt like I needed to do a longer race before the Half-Marathon, but I also knew it was more important to avoid hurting myself even more.

Listen to your body and drop down to the 5k, because if you make this worse then you definitely won't be able to do the Half-Marathon. Don't let your ego hurt your health.

Since David felt great and had no injuries, he stuck to doing the 12k. *Must be nice to be partially immortal.* At first, I was disappointed about not doing the full 12k but realized it was a waste of my time and energy to let that bring me down.

It is what it is, just do your best in the 5k.

The race was a family event. We loaded up Kaitlyn, Alex, and Grammy into the car and headed to the baseball stadium downtown. David and I used to go to football games regularly before the kiddos came along, so heading downtown for a sporting event always brings back those fond memories. There was a level of excitement back then, but nothing quite like this.

"We get to cross home plate!" I said excitedly.

"That is so cool!" my mom cheered from the back seat and snuggled in with her grandbabies. She is one of the most positive people I have ever known, and I am so thankful to have her as my mom. For years, I have described her as being like a duck; water rolls right off her back like nothing happened and she keeps moving forward. My dad is the opposite; it's easy to ruffle his feathers, and sometimes even entertaining to do it. We arrived early enough to get a close parking spot and headed to the gates at the front entrance when I spotted a familiar face.

"HEY!!!!" I cried, running up and hugging an old high school classmate. Randall smiled as I pulled him over to my family and introduced him to everyone. He had started running again and was doing the 12k.

"We were in marching band together, and I haven't seen him in 25 years!" I beamed. Band geeks will always have a connection, no matter their age.

We had plenty of time to use the bathroom and warm up before the race, and there were two different start times for the 12k and 5k. It was chilly; I was wearing pants, a long-sleeved shirt, and a pullover until it was time to run. I looked around and saw the other runners, many wearing sleeveless shirts and shorts.

"Man, I would be *freezing* wearing that!" I said and shivered at the thought.

"Yeah, but you know they'll appreciate it once they start running," David said.

"That's true, I hope I didn't make a mistake wearing this long-sleeved shirt."

"I guess you'll find out!"

My mom, kids, and I cheered for the 12k racers as they passed by and waved at us. I stood there for a minute, then decided it couldn't hurt to pee again before it was time to run. I lined up for my race and noticed a very large group of elementary school-aged kids who were running the 5k. They wore brightly colored shirts and took off running with us, and I got caught up in the sea of running children. There's nothing like young kids to keep you on your toes while racing since they go back and forth from sprinting to a dead stop without looking to see who's around them. I was trotting along when a little girl flew up behind me, passed, and then came to almost an abrupt stop directly in front of me when she ran out of gas. I jumped around her to avoid colliding, and she decided to run with me.

"I'm so tired!" she cried.

"You can do it! Just keep a steady pace with me and you won't wear out so fast!"

"Yeah...but I *wanna* run fast!" she exclaimed, and she took off.

Well, that was short-lived.

She crashed again and slowed to another walk, trying to stay with me again.

"Are you running with kids from your school?"

"Yep, I'm in second grade!"

"That's cool, my son is in first grade!"

"Why isn't he running with you?"

"He's not ready to run this far yet, but he will one day! I'll tell him all about you!"

A smile spread across her face, and I chuckled as she took off. When she crashed again, she joined a group of kids and teachers, and I waved to her as I passed by.

The route started at the baseball stadium, went across the Blossom Street bridge over the Congaree River, through Cayce, and back over the Gervais Street bridge crossing the river again. After crossing the second bridge, I slowly approached another runner who sparked my curiosity. She was running by herself at a good pace and was in her late sixties. I wanted to know her story. I struck up a short conversation and told her how I had a late start with running in my forties.

"You're right where you should be! I started running when I was 47 and haven't stopped since!"

"That gives me hope for the future!"

As I continued running, I noticed an incline ahead that was approaching the last leg of the race.

Oh my gosh, that is a steep hill, and my leg is struggling right now.

Don't give up now, you're almost there!

My inner voice chimes in most when I'm not interacting with other people around me, which makes sense because I'm not distracted. I needed it going up this hill, it was wearing me out more than expected since I didn't do a lot of hill workouts.

Just a little bit left to go, and you'll be back at the stadium to cross home plate!!

Okay, yes! I've got this!

Once I took a right turn off the hill, it leveled out and I was relieved.

There's the stadium; only a quarter mile to go!

I smiled as I approached the field, even though my leg was giving me a fit. As I turned to run into the stadium, I felt the spurt of adrenaline kick in.

I was running in the outfield, heading to the third base line. I felt like a kid again, but this time I was running on a much larger field! There wasn't enough energy left in my body for a full sprint, but I picked up the pace as I pushed through the finish line. My mom and kids were waiting, and I was a sweaty mess. It looked like wearing a long-sleeved shirt backfired.

"How was it running on the field?" my mom asked. She knew how excited I was about it.

"It was awesome! And I'm glad I didn't do the 12k distance!" I said, rubbing my sore leg.

A short time later, David made it through the finish line and was spent. The hill he had to run was significantly harder than the one I did, on top of an extra 4 ½ miles. Randall came through a few minutes later, drenched in sweat.

"Did you run through a sprinkler?!" I laughed.

"That would feel great right now, I was not expecting it to warm up that much!"

Shortly after, we piled into the car to head home, and my leg was aching and throbbing.

"I will be taking some ibuprofen when we get home!" I said, trying to massage it.

"That makes two of us," David replied.

I took a week off from running to let my leg recover and tried not to worry too much about what it would look like attempting a Half-Marathon that was quickly approaching.

We'll cross that bridge when you come to it. Let your body rest and give yourself a chance to recover.

-15-

THE NONEXISTENT PARENTING GUIDE

We decided to do our first official family event together for the Halloween 5k and Kid's Fun Run. However, I made a big boo-boo before this race. After dealing with some digestive issues, I decided to do longer intermittent fasting two days before the race. My gut immediately felt better, but I had significantly decreased my caloric intake from what my body was used to consuming. One day would have been a good gut reset, but *two* days was too much for my body. I did this close to the race because I had been overeating, and my digestive system was suffering. I'm *really* bad at eating when I'm not hungry and eating too much, which leads to digestive issues when it goes on for several days in a row. At the time, my daily fast ranged from 12-13 hours per day. If I overate one day, a longer fast to reset my gut the following day did the trick to restore the balance.

My problem with overeating was that I constantly found myself rummaging for food when I was not hungry. Even though I ate healthy food *most* of the time, it was still too much for my system to handle when I overdid it. Between staying active and incorporating daily intermittent fasting, it kept my weight under control; but it was still a struggle. Daily fasting set healthy boundaries so that I wouldn't *over*eat. My love for food had always been overwhelmingly powerful.

The morning of the race, my eyes suddenly flew open in the darkness, and I looked over at the clock that read 3:00 am.

Why am I awake? I'm not nervous about this race at all.

Then, I felt it.

Hunger.

Not the regular rumbling of your tummy that you can ignore, but a deeper rumble that was more intense than a normal hungry tummy. I got up to use the bathroom and drink some water, hoping it would distract the hunger pangs. I laid there for another two hours before I finally fell back asleep...still hungry. I woke up again at 6:20 and lay in bed like a zombie. I got up and ate a Banana Oatmeal Bar and an apple, along with some more water.

That should hold me over until after the race. Then I can indulge in a Pumpkin Cinnamon Roll Muffin and a cup of coffee when we get home.

I still decided to bring a protein shake in case I needed it. While we were on our way to the race, I could feel that I didn't get enough to eat and started to worry about crashing. When we parked, I drank the protein shake to get more calories in my system. Compared to how I normally felt before a race, I did *not* feel strong.

I want a personal best time today!

Don't worry about your time, stay steady and listen to your body.

My stubborn competitiveness was now arguing with my Yoda voice because I wanted to keep improving my overall time at *every* event. I realized there was a strong possibility that I wouldn't be able to improve this time around because of my lack of pre-fueling error. ***Note to self: don't do this again before a race. For today, do what you can. You learned from this experience, so don't dwell on it.***

Even though I wasn't feeling my best, I was still excited. Not only were our kids running their first race, but it was a Halloween event, which meant many people were dressed up. I decided to dress up as Mrs. Incredible because it was easy to get creative with this costume and perfect for the occasion. I threw on some red leggings, a red Mrs. Incredible t-shirt, thigh-high black socks, and black undies *over* my red leggings. It was perfect. It's not every day you can wear underwear *outside* your clothes and not get judged too terribly. I rolled my eyes when David claimed he was dressed up as a runner. *How original.* He preferred to save the good costumes for Halloween when he's not shooting for a personal best time, so I let it slide.

Some of the races we participate in have a chip timer for both the start *and* finish, whereas some of the smaller ones only have a chip timer for crossing the finish line. I saw that this race only had the chip activation for the finish line, so we made our way closer to the front. I learned the hard way that if you're in the far back of a race when the timer starts, you lose quite a few seconds on your time. If you're not going for a personal best, it's no big deal. If you are, it's thrown off, and I'm slightly obsessed with numbers. We lined up to the far edge behind the fast runners out of the line of fire.

I remembered watching the tortoise and the hare as a kid. Back then, it made absolutely NO sense to me how a turtle could in any way beat a rabbit in a race. I started to understand the concept of staying steady and not giving up, minus the turtle speed. Since I had set a steady pace for myself, I noticed how some people start running too fast, and then ended up wearing themselves out and I eventually passed them on the course. This race was no exception, so my turtle self just kept moving forward.

You're a Ninja Turtle, remember?

Ahh, yes. That's right. Maybe that should be my costume for next year!

The race went along relatively uneventful, other than people cheering for Mrs. Incredible who certainly didn't feel all that incredible. My strength and energy levels paid the price of not fueling properly. Although I felt decent after, there were no spurts of energy and I didn't improve my time...in fact, it was 1 second *slower* per mile. It was yet another life lesson in the books that slapped me in the face. They had a line where you could get a printout of your time and place, and when I looked at my sheet, I felt disappointed.

I could have done better.

You don't have to improve at every race. You learned a life lesson from this.

I am known for wearing my emotions all over my face and would be a terrible poker player for this reason alone. I will also be upfront and overly honest, even to strangers who ask me random questions. A woman in my age group was walking by and stopped when she saw my facial expression.

"Didn't do as well as you hoped?" she asked.

"No, I didn't eat enough the past couple of days before the race and I paid for it for today."

"Oh, is *that* why you think you didn't do well?" she said sarcastically, rolled her eyes and walked off.

I stood there in silence, shocked. I wanted to chase her down and tell her the whole story and how I was telling the truth and really didn't fuel properly.

But I'm not making excuses, that's what really happened today!

Don't worry about her. She doesn't know you, she doesn't know your story, and she doesn't have to. Let her think what she wants, it doesn't matter.

It was time for the kids to do their fun run.

KIDS' FUN RUN

The distance for a Fun Run varies at many events, and this one was a little over a quarter of a mile. Both kids had a different strategy in mind.

"I'm gonna win the whole thing!" Alex cheered with excitement.

"Oh yeah?" I replied and chuckled.

"I'm going to take it easy at first and then sprint to the end," Kaitlyn said.

I looked at her and smiled, "That is a *great* idea."

David and Grammy took the kids to the start line, while I stayed at the finish line ready to take a video. They lined up at the start when the horn blew, and all took off like jackrabbits. The Kids' Fun Runs are adorable, seeing all these little guys run their hearts out to the finish.

I saw Alex first, sprinting as fast as he could. He started out too fast, then began to slow down. Kaitlyn was running along at a steady pace, just like she said she was going to. I was focused on Alex being up front, and it looked like he would come in second place to a boy who was just ahead of him. Suddenly, Kaitlyn increased her pace and went into a full sprint. My eyes widened as I saw the amount of speed she had picked up and was gunning for the finish.

LOOK...AT...HER...

About 50 feet before the line, she *flew* past her brother. He displayed a look of shock and disappointment when she passed him, considering she took his spot of second place. My jaw dropped, then I started jumping up and down, cheering for them. My excitement had exploded. Kaitlyn had been a dancer for years, but I had no idea she had potential as a runner. I got overexcited, spiraled, and started pressing her about running while we were in the car on the ride home.

"Why don't you start running with us? They have Run Hard at your middle school, we could run 5ks as a family and you could run Track! Cross Country! You would be awesome at it! Earn a college scholarship!"

"Mom. NO! I don't want to run; I want to *dance!* I just ran today for *fun!*"

"But you would be *so* good at it!"

"I don't want to run!" she said, getting frustrated.

"Erin, just let it go," David said.

"But...."

"No, just let it go."

My shoulders slumped and I stared out the window. Our kids are complete opposites of each other. Kaitlyn is reserved, introverted, and skeptical (like David). Alex puts himself out there, is extroverted, and competitive (like me), but they are both their own versions of themselves. There are so many times when I think I'm helping one with a solution to a problem that would be more beneficial to the *other*, and vice versa.

One of the things I have struggled with as a mom is finding the balance of encouraging our kids without pushing them into retaliation. If I see potential in them, I want to provide motivation and support without overstepping boundaries and leading to resentment and burnout. It's still an art I have not mastered, especially when I see something so clearly in those kids that they don't see themselves.

Isn't that my job as a parent, to push them?

How do you respond when you're forced to do something you don't want to do?

Oh, I completely retaliate and rebel. There is no motivation there if I'm not passionate about it.

Exactly, and you want your kids to be strong and independent, right? To be what they want to be and think for themselves.

Of course, I do.

Lead by example, be a positive influence, and stay in your lane. Don't forget that. It's their life to figure out what they want, and they will do that over time.

Gosh, parenting is so rewarding and challenging at the same time. Wouldn't it be amazing if each child was born with their own parenting manual? Each one's manual would be completely different, just like me and both of my brothers.

That would be too easy. You wouldn't be challenged to grow if everything in life was too easy all the time.

Our adorable freeloaders at the Halloween 5k.

-16-

LISTENING TO MY GUT

Two weeks before the Run Hard Half-Marathon, I had an intense gut feeling I wasn't ready to complete it. Although I had been training consistently, something felt utterly wrong. Do you know that all-too-familiar gut feeling that something is off? This time, it was *powerful*.

"Come on, you can do it! I believe in you!" David said when I told him how I was feeling about it.

"Listen, I'm all about being motivated and challenging myself to see what I can do, but something doesn't feel right. I'll give it another week, but if I still feel the same way, I'll drop down to the 10k."

"Alright, do what you need to. I'm still going to do the Half-Marathon."

"I know, and I'll be waiting for you at the finish line to take a video of you winning the whole thing!"

"Right!" he laughed.

I contemplated for another week but listened to my gut and dropped down to the 10k. I wasn't happy.

No! I don't want to drop down! This is a bucket list item and I have worked hard to prepare for it!

You're not ready for a Half-Marathon yet, but you can do the 10k. It's okay to drop down, you have to do what's best for your body. Just because you don't do this one doesn't mean you won't do one in the future.

"Are you nervous about this being your first Half-Marathon?" I asked David in the car that morning on our way to the race.

"Meh, not really. I feel like I'm prepared enough to do okay. How about you?"

"I'm not nervous anymore since I dropped down to the 10k, and I'm looking forward to it."

"You'll do fine, we'll just need to get you ready for a Half-Marathon next," he smiled.

"Baby steps for big babies."

"You *are* a big baby."

"That's the pot calling the kettle black!" I laughed.

We arrived at the Lexington Blowfish Baseball Stadium just in time to avoid the road closures and grabbed a good parking spot close to the start line. This was the largest running event in Lexington, so there were hundreds of people attending as runners, volunteers, and spectators. Although the stadium was usually filled with baseball fans, this time it was buzzing with excitement for an entirely different kind of athletic event. People were scattered throughout the stadium as runners made their way in. The start line was set up on the two-lane road between the stadium and the kids' baseball complex, with three different start times for each distance. The highlight of the finish was the final stretch, which brought runners back through the stadium gates behind left field, circling over to right field, and coming down the first base line. We went into the stadium to use the bathroom, then headed back to the start line for the Half-Marathoners to line up.

"You've got this!" I cheered to David.

"Yep, I'll see you in a little while!"

I watched as he and the other runners started their portion of the race, then the rest of the 10k runners lined up next. I was feeling strong as I started running, refraining from going out too fast with all the cheers and excitement from people lining the road as we took off. The weather was perfect; it was a cool, sunny morning and the energy from the crowd was infectious. My legs moved smoothly, and I kept my breathing in sync with my strides as I ran. At events with different race routes, it's imperative to pay attention to where you're going, or you'll end up running much farther (or shorter) than you intended. I had studied the route and was very familiar with the area, so I already knew exactly where to turn, taking the navigation out of the equation to focus on the run itself.

"GO CHEF ERIN!!" I heard a female voice shout from the side of the road. It startled me and I jumped, then smiled and waved enthusiastically at her.

"I just saw your husband pass me!" I laughed.

By the time I hit mile 3, I felt like I was in a great rhythm. I was running down Hwy 378 on the edge of the far-right lane, watching as the cars zipped past us from behind. For many years, I'd heard my mom complain when people walked or ran on the wrong side of the road, with their backs to oncoming traffic.

"Don't they know how dangerous that is? They could get hit by a car!" she'd cry when she saw someone doing it (which was often). I had always been very cautious about it for that reason and heard many horror stories of people getting hit and killed.

What if these people driving down the highway don't see the cones and veer over into our lane? What if someone is distracted, or looking at their phone, and something catastrophic happens?

Stop spiraling, you'll be off this section of the road before you know it.

Three ladies passed by on my left, running together and chatting. I noticed their position, extremely close to those little cones and they didn't seem to notice the cars zipping by from behind. My anxiety spiked as I watched them.

They're too close to the edge of the lane!

They'll be okay, just focus on what's in front of you.

I still worried about them getting hit, but I also longed to run with other people at the same pace and envied how they ran together, enjoying the route. I had been invited to run with a ladies' group in the area that meets twice a week in the mornings to run 3 miles together, but two things held me back: the fear of not being able to keep up with them and running at 5:00 am in pitch black darkness. I had seen these ladies a couple of years before at a local restaurant together.

"Oh, that's a local ladies' running group, they get together a couple of times a month," someone said as I looked curiously at them. It had been so long since I had a community of close friends who got together regularly. Once motherhood entered my life and I worked from home, going out to socialize seemed almost nonexistent. And since this wasn't my hometown, it was even harder to find my people. I remember in grade school; you gravitated toward people you clicked with. As an adult, it's much more complicated. You have to find the combination of clicking with people, having schedules that don't conflict so you can see each other, living close by, being in a similar season of life (new moms versus empty nesters), or whatever other factors. Yes, it's complex as we get older, but I also needed it as an adult just as much as I needed it as a kid. I kept telling myself that I would find my people when it was meant to happen and to be patient. Going through a mid-life transformation also makes it challenging, since I'm not the same person I used to be, and not everyone who knows me understands or even accepts that.

"You need to get out and be around people, it's good for you!" my mom fussed at me regularly. She was right, but I wasn't sure what to do at the time. Now that the kids were older and I had a little more freedom to leave the house, I still yearned for the community.

If you're looking for a community, put yourself out there more often. Stop being a creampuff and step outside your comfort zone. You have to make an effort in order to see results and make a positive change.

I turned right on Wise Ferry Road at mile 4 and continued until I saw a hill in front of me. The irony was that I had been down this road well over a hundred times, but since I was driving I neglected to notice there was an incline to it; until I was running. It became painfully obvious, along with the sharp twinge in my right knee. At first, I brushed it off, thinking it was just a minor ache that would pass. As I continued up the hill, it morphed into more than a minor discomfort – it became a stabbing pain that shot through my knee every time my foot hit the ground. I tried adjusting my stride, but it didn't help. I needed to get over the incline. If I was at home running my neighborhood loop, stopping would have been easy. I was a little less than 2 miles from the finish line, and I refused to walk. I had come too far to slow down to walk, and my stubbornness was strong. The idea of pushing through seemed impossible until I made it over the incline and the road leveled. Although the pain lessened, it didn't go away as I continued to run.

My knee is killing me!!
Get to the finish line, you can do this.

When I made it back to Ball Park Road, there was a strong mix of feelings between fatigue, pain, and motivation. The finish line was not far, and there was no way I was giving up this close to the end. I let the motivation take over to drive me to the stadium. As I rounded out the last part of the road course and made my way into the outfield, pure joy took over. I picked up my pace as I ran from left field to right field, then took a right to go down the first base line toward the finish. As I ran toward the line in front of me, I smiled big for the camera and thought about my main goal for races; to finish with a smile on my face.

My knee certainly didn't feel like smiling, but my soul did. I loved this race. I loved the feeling of being able to run 6.2 miles without stopping for the first time. I loved the progress I made and had no regrets about not completing the Half-Marathon. I was thankful to have listened to my gut because I couldn't have imagined how much worse it would have been if I had run another seven miles with my knee in the shape it was. My ego took a back seat to my intuition.

I walked around slowly after finishing, chatting with people I knew, and munched on a snack while I waited for David to finish his first Half-Marathon. I kept checking my phone for his location, eagerly anticipating his arrival. When I cheered for him coming down the main road, I quickly moved back into the stadium to greet him at the finish line. I know this man well enough to know when he is struggling, and he was *really* struggling.

"Congratulations!! Are you doing okay?" I asked after he crossed the finish line and slowly made his way through the stands. I mixed a packet of Liquid IV into a cold bottle of water and handed it to him.

"Gimme a minute."

Having been together since 2004, I know when to give him space, and that was one of those times. I quietly stayed close by as he walked around slowly, sipping the water bottle and recovering from the run.

"Do you want me to drive home?" I asked.

"If you don't mind."

"No problem. You ready to leave now?"

"Yes, please."

On the ride home, it took him a few minutes to cool off and regain the energy to morph back into his human form.

"So, how was it?"

"That was *tough*!!" he replied, exasperated.

"I'm sure it was, it would've been extremely bad if I had done that distance today!"

"I'll be more prepared for the next Half-Marathon in Myrtle Beach."

"I have no doubt you will," I smiled at him.

My soul was smiling, but my knee was screaming.

-17-

MID-LIFE CRISIS

For many people, a midlife crisis conjures images of sports cars or impulsive changes. As the kids grow more independent, and the days of constant parenting demands begin to ease, an unsettling feeling creeps in—questions about purpose, identity, and whether life had peaked or if something more was out there. Growing up, I heard many people talk about having a mid-life crisis. I didn't understand it very much at the time, I just knew that people in their forties lost their minds and did something totally bonkers.

My mom started taking an annual girls' trip in her early forties when I was in middle school, so I figured that was hers. It was pretty subtle, which goes along with her personality. I loved that she had so much fun and understood as an adult how important those trips still are to this day, but as a teenager, I loathed it when she went out of town because I missed her.

My dad had an older Corvette that he bought when I was in first grade and kept for a couple of years. I rode with him to pick up Robbie, who was in seventh grade, from school. All his friends were standing with him as we pulled up in the Corvette, and he started jumping up and down with excitement as his friends stared in awe at the car. I smiled at their reaction because I understood their excitement.

Since I was 2 years old, I was completely in love with sports cars (getting a minivan as a mom was a gut punch to my soul). I had a large, framed picture of a white Lamborghini Countach over my bed until Michael had some friends over and knocked the picture off the wall, destroying it. My little heart was crushed. When I was fourteen, my mom and I hopped in the car one evening to run to the grocery store. As we approached the entrance of our neighborhood, I saw a brand-new sports car pulling in from the highway. It was a Pontiac Firebird Formula, bright red with dark tinted windows, T-tops, and a deep, throaty V8 engine that roared every time you hit the gas pedal.

"There's Daddy in his new car!" she exclaimed.

My eyes almost popped out of my head.

"WHAT?!?!?!" I cried.

My poor mom. She stopped the car as he pulled up, and I jumped out. I ran over to the car, circling it, jumping up and down, and squealing like a 4-year-old.

"Stop screaming and get in, I don't want you to get hit by another car pulling up!" he yelled.

I happily obliged and jumped in. He turned the car around at the neighborhood entrance and pulled back out onto the median of the highway.

"You ready?" he asked with a smile.

"YES!!!"

He hit the gas pedal, and we took off. The car engine roared as we accelerated faster than any car I had ever ridden in. I felt my stomach jump up in my throat, and I squealed with delight. For many years, my brothers and I have picked on our dad about how slow he drives...unless he's accelerating. He takes off like a cheetah yet slows down to the speed of a sloth, traveling under the speed limit and people getting stuck behind him. My teenage heart was in love with the car, and that heart broke in half when he traded it in for a truck...just two weeks before I got my driver's license.

"I know what my mid-life crisis is," I said to David as the thought hit me.

"Uh-oh, what's that?"

"Running."

He laughed.

"What? I'm serious!"

"Well, I guess it's better than what a lot of people go through as a mid-life crisis."

"Is it though? Sometimes I feel like it's an obsession, with my OCD kicking in full force. You know how I get super excited about something, then completely overdo it and end up hurting myself...then give up. I have to find a healthy balance."

"Yeah, you are pretty bad about that," he agreed.

I can always count on him for honesty, in both good and bad situations. He will often tell me what I don't want to hear, but in most cases, I *need* to hear it. **That is required for growth.**

Fear and anxiety had kept me sitting in my comfort zone for too long. After the last 10k, I didn't run for seven weeks. Between giving my knee some time to rest and feeling somewhat emotionally defeated, it seemed like a good time to take a break and reassess my goals. However, I refused to give up. After coming so far from what I thought was never an option in my life, I saw a light of hope that I didn't think existed. Becoming an elite runner wasn't on the table, but stepping outside that comfort zone to see what I was capable of accomplishing had become the main focus. At first, running was a way to get out of the house and have a break from the endless to-do lists and routines. As I started to hit the pavement often, it became something else entirely. Running had given me a sense of control and accomplishment that had been missing for a long time. It wasn't about losing weight or competing; it was about progressing in something I thought was impossible for so long. Each mile was like peeling back a layer of doubt, frustration, and the feeling of being lost in the roles of "mom" and "wife."

What started as an escape became an obsession. I started doing things that felt unthinkable. It wasn't just the physical challenge, though that part was empowering; it was the sense of reclaiming something personal, something just for me. As the miles piled up, so did the confidence. I started testing my limits and discovering strengths I didn't know I had. For me, running wasn't about chasing youth or escaping age. It was about reinventing myself amid a life that felt settled and predictable. It became a way to remind myself that growth doesn't stop at a certain age and that midlife doesn't have to be a crisis—it can be a transformation.

Running had given me a sense of freedom and purpose I hadn't realized I was missing, and I embraced this new chapter of my life with open arms. What says "mid-life crisis" like willingly signing up to sweat profusely and gasp for breath in public? Sometimes I felt like my training gear had begun to take over the house like a strange mid-life explosion. It all started innocently with a new pair of running shoes, but my wardrobe had turned into a factory that contained a collection of moisture-wicking shirts along with matching pants or shorts, and don't forget about the compression socks to go along with those new running shoes. I had carefully curated playlists to get me pumped up for training and races and relied on my GPS watch that tracked heart rate, pace, and possibly the weather on Mars. But, I am still convinced this is the best mid-life crisis ever.

-18-

HOMETOWN HALF

Over time, New Year's Resolutions lost their appeal since mine seemed to be the same as everyone else's; to lose the weight I gained during the holidays. With the amount of food I ate between Halloween and New Year's Eve every year, you would have thought I was a pregnant grizzly bear eating enough to prepare for six months of hibernation. It was bad. At some point, I realized that resolutions rarely stuck, so I shifted my focus to yearly *goals* instead. It felt more practical, realistic, and within reach. I could map out my goals across the entire year, giving myself time to achieve them. When January rolled around, it was time to revisit those goals and get back into training. Completing a Half-Marathon was still high on my list. It was a big challenge, and I wanted it—badly.

When I started looking at races, I came across the Myrtle Beach Marathon. It is an annual event held in early March and attracts runners from all over the country. It's known for having a flat and fast course and is a favorite for runners who are aiming for personal best times or qualifying for the Boston Marathon. The course offers scenic views of downtown Myrtle Beach, Market Common, Ocean Boulevard, the Atlantic Ocean, and the Myrtle Beach Boardwalk. In addition to the full marathon, it also has a Half-Marathon, 5k, and Family

Fun Run making it accessible to runners of all ages and abilities.

Growing up in Surfside Beach, the thought of doing my first big race in the area of my hometown was exciting. However, I had to be prepared. For this race, there's a time limit of 3 hours and 15 minutes to complete the 13.1 miles. Although my 5k pace per mile was just under 11 minutes, that's for 3.1 miles. When you throw another *ten* miles on top of that, it changes things drastically. I had a lot of work to do, so I started training again regularly, slowly building up my mileage. The longest distance I completed before the big day was 10 miles, and that was only once.

You've trained enough to complete the distance, so let's see what you've got.

Two weeks before the race, the only feelings I had rolling around in my gut were nervousness and excitement. I felt ready this time around, unlike how I felt about it a few months earlier. On the day of the race, my eyes flew open in the darkness, and I rolled over to look at the clock which read 2:15 am.

Are you serious? These race nerves are getting ridiculously annoying. Maybe I can go back to sleep for a couple of hours.

The time ticked by as I lay in bed, staring at the ceiling and thinking about the day ahead. I still didn't have any dread or negative gut feelings, but I had some other emotions flowing around. Although I was still nervous and excited, I was also annoyed because it really would have been nice to have slept another couple of hours before getting up to eat my breakfast. When I looked at the clock again and saw it was almost 4:00, I gave up trying to go back to sleep and quietly pulled myself out of bed. I fumbled around in the darkness, putting on a pair of pants and a pullover to protect myself from the freezing temperature I insisted on setting the thermostat when it was time for bed in the evening.

"Why are you always trying to freeze me out at night?" David had complained on numerous occasions.

"It's good sleeping temperature!"

The man doesn't have much fat for natural insulation, so the combination of that and me being a hot sleeper is another reason we are yin and yang. However, he would rather be cold than wake up in a sweat. I made my way into the kitchen and grabbed two bottles of water, an LMNT packet, a protein shake, and an oatmeal bar. As I sat on the couch to commence my pre-race meal regimen, I pulled out the laptop and looked over the race website to look at the route again.

This will be a different way of cruising the boulevard than what I was used to.

I chuckled to myself as memories of driving down the boulevard hundreds of times in high school and college with friends. One time in particular, my best friend and I were sitting in traffic with Snoop Dogg blaring as loud as the volume would go in my red Mustang with the windows rolled down. Two police officers flew up next to us on a golf cart and looked in the car, shocked to see two college girls.

"What are you listening to?!" one officer asked.

My eyes widened as I carefully turned down the volume, and replied in a small voice, "Snoop Dogg!"

They told me to keep the volume down and drove off. My bestie and I looked at each other, laughed hysterically, and kept the volume down just a little bit.

"How long have you been up?" David sleepily asked when he walked into the living room and headed for his caffeine elixir-making machine.

"You don't wanna know."

"That bad?"

"Well, I got five solid hours of sleep, so it's enough to get me through the race."

We went through our routine of getting ready while David's mom (Mimi), Alex, and Kaitlyn slept in their rooms. We were staying in a condo for the weekend and made it a birthday getaway trip since David's birthday was the day before the race.

Who would want to run 13.1 miles on their birthday weekend? Most people wouldn't, but we're obviously nuts.

As we drove to Myrtle Beach from Pawleys Island in the darkness, there was very little traffic on the road. This time of morning, the normally congested Grand Strand looked like a sparsely populated ghost town with hardly any other drivers.

"I wonder how many of these people are up for the day, and how many are just finishing their night?"

"I'm sure it's a good mix of both," he replied.

"I can't imagine partying all night like I did in college," I said, reminiscing the days of staying out until 5:00 am, and very thankful that smartphones and social media didn't exist back then.

"Nope, we're too old for that!"

"I value sleep way too much these days!"

When we approached 21st Avenue North, we saw streams of cars heading into the parking lots at

Broadway at the Beach. There were headlights and taillights everywhere, searching for parking spaces around the construction areas.

"I'm pretty sure these people are *starting* their day running, not finishing it," I laughed.

We found a parking spot and triple-checked to make sure we had everything we needed before we locked the car and walked through the parking lot. We walked past a lone port-o-potty in the construction area and saw a few people waiting nearby. I contemplated jumping in line until one guy came out of it.

"Somebody partied too hard and got sick in there, it's all over the walls," he told the other people who were waiting. A few guys laughed, and a couple of ladies changed their minds and exited the line. I shuddered at the thought of going in there and seeing the walls decorated with vomit.

Nope, nope, and NOPE. Keep on walking.

We crossed the road and made our way to the start line close to the Myrtle Beach Pelicans Baseball Stadium. As we approached an open field off to the side, my mouth dropped, and I stared in awe at the largest number of port-o-potties I had ever seen in my life with hundreds of people waiting in lines to use them.

"Holy cow!" I cried.

"Yeah, I'd hate to wait in that line."

"Well..." I said sheepishly.

"Don't tell me you need to pee again!"

"Don't tell me you're surprised!"

"How much water did you drink?"

"I was only going to drink *two* bottles, but I decided on a third one. That was probably a mistake."

As we waited in line, I noticed some serious female runners in front of us. You could tell by their lean physique and running gear that the only way we mere mortals could keep up with them was if we were on a golf cart. They were discussing the Boston Marathon.

"Are you qualifying for Boston again today?"

"I'm already going since I ran it last year and qualified again; I'm here because I love *this* race!"

I stared at these centaurs in awe, then looked at David and whispered, "Did you hear that?? They're a few years *older* than me, too!"

The Boston Marathon was established in 1897 and is the world's oldest annual marathon. It is also one of the most prestigious races globally since it requires runners to meet strict qualifying times based on age and gender, which ensures a highly competitive field. It's not a race you can randomly get into, you have to *earn* your spot to be there, and includes the fastest marathoners in the world.

"One day, that'll be us," he said with a smile.

"I wish! I doubt they allow turtle joggers."

We made it out of the port-o-potties just in time to hear an announcer saying it was almost time to start.

"We need to hurry! We don't want to miss it!"

"We're not going to miss it; the chips record our time when we start!" he reminded me.

As we approached the start line, there was a sea of people both ahead of and behind us. I searched the crowd for anyone I knew and spotted a familiar face.

"Hey, Ed!" I called out and waved to local weatherman Ed Piotrowski when I saw him walking to the start line. He's a local celebrity around Myrtle Beach,

ABC 15's chief meteorologist, and has spent over 30 years in the coastal Carolinas. His wife is a runner, and they do many events together. He even organizes a yearly 5k in early June called Ed's Hurricane Hustle. My mom and I follow his Facebook page for weather updates, hilarious quotes, and inspirational posts.

"Hey!" He smiled and waved back, even though he had no clue who I was. He's most likely used to strangers saying hello like he is their bestie.

We were a quarter mile from the start line when the gun went off and watched the ocean of people shift from being a motionless wave to a flowing tsunami. We picked up our walking pace as we got closer, then started jogging just before we crossed the start line. I had already taken some video clips, so I whipped out my phone again and recorded before we split up.

"I'll run with you for a little while," David said.

"No, you go ahead!"

I think he felt guilty leaving me, but I would have felt worse holding him back from completing his goal. He was looking to improve his time from the last Half-Marathon he did in November, and we would eventually run together. I fully expected to be slow that day, because for me, it was all about simply finishing the race.

You both have your own goals, with running and life in general. You're at the race together, and that is what matters!

About a half mile in, I felt sloshing around in my belly from consuming too much water in a short period of time before running.

Dang, I should not have had that extra bottle of water! This is really uncomfortable!

I eased my jog just a little, to see if that would help alleviate the discomfort. A few minutes went by, and it settled. For the many years that I lived there and experienced so much of what Myrtle Beach has to offer, I had never seen it from this perspective, running along Hwy 17 Business. My parents owned and operated a riverboat company on the Intracoastal Waterway from 1990-2011 from the south end of the beach at the Waccatee Zoo and also Barefoot Landing in North Myrtle Beach. I knew the area like the back of my hand.

At mile 4, I could tell by the people around me that we were leisurely runners, moving at a slow jog or fast walk. I could only assume they were on a similar journey as me looking to complete the race, or they just loved doing it. Either way, they were out there. As I made the right turn headed into the old Air Force Base toward Market Common, I saw the faster runners coming out and going to Ocean Boulevard. It blew my mind how much farther ahead they were.

They're on a different journey than you. It's not impossible for you to eventually get there, but it's not the reason you're here today. You're out here to see what YOU are capable of doing, not anyone else.

As I daydreamed of one day morphing into one of those centaurs, I passed a couple of people I went to Socastee High School with. Although I called their names, they had earbuds packed into their ears, presumably blasting the theme song from *Rocky* based on how fast they were going and couldn't hear me.

Look for the handsome fella with dark hair wearing an orange shirt. He's a keeper.

"HEY!!" We both cried and waved as we passed.

I was taking a video while looking for him, and I commented that this was the *only* way I would be passing my husband on the course. I approached the turnaround point in Market Common and the urge to empty my bladder became intense. There were a few port-o-potties, but there was a line.

I don't want to wait in line!

You'll pass by them again after you turn around, maybe the line will be gone by then.

About half a mile down the road was the turnaround, so I crossed my fingers and toes that there wouldn't be a line when I came by the second time. The closer I got, the stronger the urge became, and knew that I risked peeing myself if I didn't stop very soon. I rounded a slight curve, and they came into my sight, with no one waiting to use them.

YES!!!

I hopped inside and shut the door. The amount of sweat produced by my body had soaked into my capris, but I was able to pull them down and let out a loud sigh of relief as my bladder emptied. When I stood up and attempted to pull up my pants, I quickly discovered that it was like I was stuffing a jumbo marshmallow into a toaster. My race pants are one size smaller than my training pants, and this is because the training pants are more comfortable; but they inch down when I run longer. For races, I can handle being stuffed into a smaller size to avoid constantly pulling them up while running, so it's a give-and-take. In the moments when I'm trying to pull the smaller-sized pants over sweaty thighs, it becomes a maneuvering obstacle.

I bent my legs down and pulled the pants up from the knees, but they refused to cooperate. I jumped a couple of times, attempting to wrestle the pants into submission and shaking the port-o-potty. I could only imagine what someone was thinking if they were standing outside waiting on me, hearing a huge sigh of relief, then seeing it wobble with a bang each time my feet landed from jumping to pull my pants back up. About fifteen seconds later, I finally peeled my pants from my thighs to cover my hips and waist, double-checked to make sure there wouldn't be a wardrobe malfunction I may have missed, exited the port-o-potty, and got back on the road.

Trotting down Ocean Boulevard, I passed mile 8 and noticed the spectators that were sprinkled along the sidewalks watching us as we went by. Many had signs or cheered, and I overheard a man talking loudly to the people around him. They were sitting in their fold-out chairs, watching us run by.

"Yeah, I think these are the half-marathoners because the *good* runners are upfront and probably done by now," he said.

Without thinking, I responded immediately.

"Yep, they are! *Thank you!!*" I cried with a combined tone of cheerfulness and sarcasm.

The runners around me who heard the exchange laughed and thanked me for saying something to him. I figured he didn't think he was talking loud enough for everyone else to hear him because his face dropped, and he became silent. I chuckled and shook my head.

"We're running faster than *he* is!" exclaimed a woman next to me.

"That's right!" I laughed.

You don't have to be an elite runner to participate in a race. Most who are out there are average people who challenge themselves to grow or try something new. I love the diversity of runners I see at events, with people of all shapes, sizes, and ages. I used to think that all runners had to be young and thin, but I learned quickly that's not the case when I saw people twice my size and age outrunning me on many occasions. Sometimes you could tell if someone was a fast runner, while other times you would be blown away with shock to see what they could do...and I *loved* it.

As I was jogging down the boulevard watching the cars pass by, I saw a car that stood out. It was red, sleek, and coming towards us. I stared at it as it got closer, then gasped.

THAT'S A LAMBORGHINI!!!!!

My face lit up as I grabbed my phone, fumbling to pull it out of my pocket as quickly as I could to take a picture just as it passed by. My inner child was jumping up and down, squealing with excitement. A few minutes later and almost to mile 10, the pain started sinking in when I suddenly felt a familiar pang.

Hunger.

Oh no, it's not a normal one, either. I have waited too long and now it feels like my blood sugar is dropping quickly. This is not good.

I dug around in my pocket and pulled out a S'mores flavored Gu gel. Although I wasn't a huge fan of the ingredients (basically pure sugar), I knew I needed something to help me through it. I had only packed two gels for the entire route, which was a big mistake on my end since I was out there for so long. The general rule of thumb is to take in calories every 45-60 minutes during a long endurance race, and I was already at 2 ½ hours.

Time slipped away, go ahead and take in the gel to increase your energy levels.

I sucked down the first gel and chased it with water. It was delicious and gave me some energy, but at this point, the damage was done by waiting too long to fuel. I still had over three miles to go. Fifteen minutes later, I had to take the second gel.

Oh no, what if I run out of energy? Can I make it to the finish line?

Sip your water and keep moving. You have come so far; you can make it!

Okay, focus.

At this point, I had been walking and jogging equally on and off the entire route, and I was cutting it very close to the time limit of 3 hours and 15 minutes.

There are still plenty of people behind you, they're not going to kick everyone off.

I remembered seeing the last person making their way into the old Air Force base when we were coming out. I knew they were the last racers because a police escort followed them, and regular traffic was moving slowly behind the police.

You're getting close to the skywheel!

I was excited to see the skywheel for a couple of reasons. First, I loved to see it because it's been a landmark of Myrtle Beach for many years. Second, it was close to the turn to finish the last leg of the race. As I approached the skywheel, I saw the signs that separated the route from the half-marathon to the marathon.

Those who were going the full 26.2 miles continued straight, while the rest of us turned left to head back to the finish line. I was nowhere near ready for a full marathon and was happy to take that turn. I loved this as an option for people who were unable to do the full route. It is on my radar as a possible future marathon attempt, and this is one of the main reasons. If someone registers to do the full marathon but realizes at the halfway point it's not their day to do it, they have the option to cut it short.

As I approached the turn, I saw a female runner around my age passed out on the sidewalk. I gasped and slowed down when I saw her, but realized the paramedics had just gotten there to help as I got closer. She was unconscious at first but started to come to as they transferred her to a stretcher and into the ambulance. My heart hurt for her.

Did she get dehydrated?

My mom, grandmother, and I all started dealing with dehydration issues in our late thirties. My grandmother only drank coffee and sweet tea, and as she got older her dehydration issues intensified. She passed out from dehydration semi-regularly, going to the hospital each time. My mom passed out a few years ago in the heat, and I have come close a few times as well. I became neurotic about hydration since I started running to avoid this lovely phenomenon.

David teases me because I keep electrolyte packets in my purse during the summer, always have a bottle of water with me everywhere I go and pee a lot because of it. I'd rather be looking for a bathroom to relieve my bladder than be laid up in a hospital bed hooked to an IV. The irony is that he needs one of those electrolyte packets after races because that has happened to him a few times. *Mm-hmm.*

At first, I passed the ambulance as it was loading her up, and then it passed me on its way to the hospital. I didn't know if that's what happened to her, but it is why I take so many precautions to stay hydrated before, during, and after running.

Ain't nobody got time to be laid up in a hospital.

I sipped on my water as I thought about it, and hoped she was okay. At this point, I was struggling on a level I had never experienced. The tops of my feet hurt tremendously, an intense pain I hadn't felt before.

What is that? Why does it hurt so much?

You're almost there, look! Mile 12 ahead!

Okay, good. Just a little over a mile to go.

I felt a small amount of adrenaline course through my veins at the thought of being so close to the finish line and picked up speed, but it didn't last long when the pain came searing back with more intensity.

My feet have never hurt like this. What's going on? Are they going to fall off?

Think about it, you've never run this far, you didn't fuel properly, and your body is wearing out. Make it to the finish line, then you can rest.

I continued at a jog, trying to ignore the pain with very little success, but kept moving forward. I truly felt like a turtle. By the time I hit the last half mile of the course, I was completely spent, and the tops of my feet felt like they were being stabbed by little knives with every step I took.

This hurts SO much more than my knee did during the 10k!!
But you're SO close!
Okay, I've got this. I can do this. The finish line is right around the corner.

As I turned left off Robert Grissom Parkway, the last section of the race was packed with spectators. Coming from the other direction were runners finishing the full marathon while I was finishing the half. I stared at them in awe and wondered why they weren't wearing superhero capes because they were gliding in like they just went for a leisurely run in the park while I felt like I needed to be rolled in on a gurney. I took the last right turn, and a short burst of adrenaline came through to give me a small amount of energy to make it to the finish line to see my time.

3:15:56
Oh no! I didn't make it under 3:15!
YOU DID IT!! YOU COMPLETED A HALF MARATHON!! Check that *off your* bucket list!!

My inner voice was more excited than I was because all I wanted to do was take my shoes off and lay down for the next twelve years.

"Congratulations!" David smiled and hugged me. "How did you do?"

"Well, I think my feet are about to disintegrate, but I made it through the finish line! I need to get a bottle of water and sit down, I'm in a *lot* of pain."

We walked over to the baseball field where everyone was either lying on the ground or celebrating their achievement. I loosened the laces on my shoes and felt instant relief. We relaxed for a few minutes, then grabbed our race shirts and headed for the car. There was some ibuprofen in there that was calling my name.

"You did it! You finished your first Half-Marathon! How do you feel?" David asked.

"Physically, I'm struggling."

I sat there for a few seconds and thought about it. Then, I smiled and said, "Emotionally, I feel fantastic! I can't believe I made it through! A Half-Marathon! I *never* thought I could do that!! Like, *ever*!!!"

I pulled my shoes off and looked at my feet, which were bright red and felt like they had been pounded down with a meat mallet.

"I'd like to figure out what's going on with my feet though, I have never felt pain like that before and thought I was more prepared."

After consulting Doctor Google, it looked as though I dealt with a case of extensor tendonitis that went away after a few days of rest. This is common for runners who suddenly increase their running load and/or don't have the right footwear. In this case, my shoelaces were excruciatingly tight for a long run that my body wasn't used to. Case closed.

"Ready to sign up for the full marathon next year?" He asked.

I pulled up the internet on my phone.

"What are you doing?"

"I'm ordering a straitjacket and am going to tie you up in it while you're asleep."

He laughed, but I was only half-joking.

Well, you never thought you could complete a Half-Marathon, who says you can't eventually be ready for a full in the future?

Be still, my heart.

So far, the hardest medal I had earned.

-19-

CROSSING THE BRIDGE

"I'd love to do the Cooper River Bridge Run in Charleston this year," David piped up one evening after dinner while looking for other races.

"It's only 2 months away, but I'm up for it if you can find a hotel. Do you know how *huge* that race is? About 30,000 people go every year, and it's a madhouse with finding a hotel," I replied.

"I'll look and see what I can find."

Michael did a little bit of running with friends for a couple of years in his twenties, and this was his favorite race. He would do a couple of 5k races in preparation, but this was his event of choice and ran it several times. Since I'm always trying to get other people to drink the Crazy Juice and run with me, I called him to see if he and his son would be interested in coming along with us. Zack was in 8th grade and ran track for his middle school, and his mom, Tracy, had been walking regularly for the past couple of months.

"Hey, we're going to do the Cooper River Bridge Run, would y'all be interested in coming with us?"

"Oh, I *love* that race, but it's been 25 years. I need to start training, but it's worth it," he said, presumably reminiscing about his short-lived glory days.

"Well then, start training! There you go, problem solved. What other issues should we tackle?"

"Coming from the running freak, of course, you and David will have no problems with it. The rest of us normal people need to be prepared!"

"We're related. You're *not* normal."

"Good point. Let me think about it and talk with Tracy and Zack. I'll call you back."

A few minutes later, he called back.

"We'd all like to do it; but Tracy and I will walk. Have you already gotten a hotel? I know how hard it is to find a place for that weekend."

"Yep, David already found a place, just waiting on you to find out if y'all are coming with us to book it."

He laughed, "Y'all aren't messing around with this, are you?"

"Nope! You know I'm a planner, and he really wants to do this one! We found a place in Mount Pleasant that will hold all of us."

"Yep, book it."

Checkmate: they drank the Crazy Juice.

"When you register for the race, you'll register as a walker or runner. If you can run it in *under* one hour, you have to upload previous race times, so they know where to place you in the corrals. You have to provide evidence that you're as fast as you say you are."

"Are you serious? Wow, it's grown a lot since the last time I did it," he said.

"Well, you *are* getting old."

"Thank you, I am well aware of this."

"You're welcome! Just wanted to make sure you didn't forget. That's what little sisters are for."

I looked forward to running over the new bridge that had been built since I participated in college.

The Cooper River Bridge Run is one of the largest and most popular road races in the United States that brings in people from all over the world. The start line is in Mount Pleasant and crosses over the Arthur Ravenel Jr. Bridge (built in 2005), finishing in downtown Charleston. The race originally started in 1978 with 766 finishers and has grown exponentially over the years.

The first time I participated in the race was in 1999. My mom's sister, Ellen, lived in Summerville with her daughters, so we spent the weekend with them. My mom and aunt were fit enough to walk the 6.2 miles. I was 18, and always excited to take a trip to see my cousins. Rhi is two years younger than me, and Aja is just five weeks older. Rhi's social calendar was filled to the rim even as a teenager, which meant she wasn't home much on the weekends. I could strongly relate, considering we both have similar outgoing personalities. Her sister, Aja, is quite the opposite. She was happy to spend time at home curled up on the couch with a good book, and we shared a similar love of music. I remember listening to Tears for Fears in the mid-eighties at our grandparents' house in the living room, talking about how much we loved the song, "Everybody Wants To Rule The World."

I've heard that cousins are your first best friends, and my relationship with Aja would prove that theory correct. She is a reserved introvert; she and I clicked from the very beginning. She is the sister I never had but always wanted, and we joke to this day that she and I may have been switched at birth. Her personality is similar to my mom's, and my personality is more similar to her mom's. We can go months without seeing each other, but when we get together it's like no time has passed. "I'm going to call Aja really quick," often turns into a two-hour phone call full of laughter and sometimes tears when the conversations go deep as we solve the world's problems together. I refer to our conversations as therapy sessions, although I am convinced she's more of *my* therapist than I am of hers. It's also hard not to develop a close relationship with someone you took childhood baths with for years. We have a few blackmail-worthy pictures of us, naked and smiling as toddlers in the tub together. Although I couldn't convince Aja to walk the Cooper River Bridge event with me, we spent quality time together before and after the race.

Six miles? No problem.

I was in decent shape, but mostly...I was *eighteen*. I didn't have to run the race. Most people walked so I didn't train. I attempted to jog a few times along the route, but I walked most of the way. Endurance running was not my gig, even as a teenager. What I remember most about it back then was the last mile. This was before the event reached a gazillion participants, so it wasn't the madhouse it is today. The last mile was phenomenal; everyone was spaced out with plenty of room to run, and the adrenaline rush that surged through my body from all the people lining the streets and cheering was overpowering.

Honestly, I think that is the hardest I had ever run in my life. In the last quarter mile, people were so amped up and cheering that I broke into a full sprint. When they saw me do this, they cheered louder...and I ran *harder*. My lungs screamed at me along with the burning in my legs, but it was a dopamine hit I had never experienced and didn't want to stop. When I crossed the finish line, I thought I was going to collapse from running so hard. I quickly found some water and grabbed every item of free food I could get my grubby little hands on. Let's face it, my teenage metabolism and resiliency could handle it back then with no problem.

Give me a dozen donuts, I deserve it!

The following year, we did the race again. Only that time, I wanted to train for it. When I told my best friend about it, she wanted to participate as well, so we "trained" together. I say "trained" lightly because we had no idea what we were doing and only did a few random jogging intervals while walking together in our neighborhood. At the race, we trotted along together at a slow pace, jogging when we could before slowing down to a walk and repeating, while taking in the scenery and chatting. She and I were inseparable; we lived together, worked together, socialized together, and went to the same college. You'd think we would have run out of things to talk about, but that never happened. She was my favorite person for many years.

When we made it to the incline of the bridge, we saw a little girl ahead of us who looked to be about 7 years old, and she was alone. We looked at each other.

"Is she by herself?" she asked me.

"I don't know, it looks like it."

We continued to watch her as she walked up the bridge. We both kept looking around for anyone else who might be with her, but there was no one.

"Hey, are you by yourself?" I asked as we came up on either side of her.

"Yeah, I don't know where my family is."

My bestie and I looked at each other, worried.

"Your family is here though, right?"

"I was with my grandma and cousins, but I lost them and can't find them anywhere."

We nodded at each other, then slowed down to walk with her.

"Would you like us to stay with you until you find your family?" I asked.

"Yes!!"

"Okay!"

We kept her entertained and talked to her throughout the rest of the route, playing silly games while looking for her family. She wanted to run a few times with us, so we would all speed up together at a sprint before inevitably slowing down again, laughing.

"This is fun!" she cried.

When we got to the finish line, we loaded up on drinks and snacks as we looked for her family.

"Do you want to get on my shoulders so you can see around a little better?" I asked.

"Yes!"

I picked her up, put her on my shoulders, and walked around the sea of people, looking for her family. As a kid, I loved sitting on my dad's or brothers' shoulders because it felt like I was on top of the world. I would suddenly be way taller than I had ever been, and the world looked different with a full-range view of everything around me. I felt a mix of excitement and nervousness as I giggled and gripped their head to steady myself, squealing when one of them pretended they were going to fall; which they did *often*.

After almost an hour of walking around, I noticed

the time. We were late for meeting up with my mom, and I knew she would be worried to pieces if she couldn't find us. This was during the Jurassic Period before cell phones, so we had to rely on watches and meet-up times.

"We have to go, but we're not going to leave you by yourself. How about we take you to this police officer over here?"

"Okay!" she smiled.

I took her off my shoulders and we held her hands as we walked over to the officer to explain what happened and how we still couldn't find her family.

"Thank you, I'll take care of it!" he said as he took her hand and squatted down to talk to her.

"Bye, it was nice to meet you!"

"Bye!" she smiled and waved.

On race day, I set my alarm for 5:00 am, but my excitement woke me up around 4:00. I lay in bed and stared at the clock, my anticipation building.

This will be great; you can base your 10k time on this race for the future.

I'm not a big fan of comparing every race event just by the distance since so many courses are different. Running the 10k in Lexington didn't include the 1-mile steep elevation of climbing the bridge, and it certainly didn't have a huge crowd of people to bob and weave if I got a spurt of energy. No, this race was special.

We stayed at the Residence Inn in a 2-bedroom suite. David and I were in one bedroom, Michael and Tracy in the other, and Zack on the pull-out sofa in the living area. I quietly tiptoed into the dark living area from our room to eat my oatmeal bar and drink a protein shake, followed by two bottles of water. It was almost pitch black since I was trying to avoid waking up my sleeping nephew by not turning on any lights. Thankfully, my eyes were adjusted enough to where I could eat and drink without spilling or dropping anything; but I'm convinced that most teenagers could sleep through a typhoon. Although he and I harassed each other relentlessly, I wanted to make sure he got enough sleep before running.

"You are the sleep police," David has told me regularly.

"Yes, I am! Having kids and losing a significant amount of sleep made me realize how precious it is, and I don't want to take that away from anyone! Ever!"

"Uh-huh."

"Oh please, I know you appreciate sleep, considering you need a pot of coffee before you become human in the morning."

Since becoming a mom, I started monitoring bedtime schedules like a drill sergeant, calculating exactly how many hours of sleep they needed to avoid meltdowns (both mine and theirs). Parenthood introduced a whole new level of exhaustion I never knew existed. Staying up until 2:00 am was no longer on the table if I was unable to get enough sleep, and when I heard about someone else sleeping 14 hours straight, I imagined snoozing uninterrupted on a bed of feathers in the clouds. These days, I'm lucky to sleep 7 hours straight without waking up at least once.

It was kind of depressing sitting there in the darkness. I hoped somebody would wake up soon but was sure it wouldn't be Zack. He'd be the last one who wanted to wake up. He rustled around on the pull-out sofa, and I froze.

Did I wake him up? No, he's still out.

I heard David shuffle out of bed and into the bathroom, so it wouldn't be long before everyone else started moving around.

It's about time, I feel like a vampire sitting in this dark room by myself, waiting to pounce on an unsuspecting victim.

Michael walked out of their bedroom quietly, until he noticed that I was sitting alone in the dark and starting laughing.

"What are you doing??"

"I woke up early and had to eat something before we ran, but I didn't want to wake him up!"

"Hey, it's time to get up!" he raised his voice.

Zack groaned as he started moving.

"But I don't wanna!" he whined.

"You sound like your mother!"

"She probably didn't sleep well because of your snoring," I chimed in.

"That is correct!" Tracy cried from their room.

After everyone got up and ready, we hopped in the car and drove to a grocery store parking lot in Mount Pleasant, close to the corrals. The day before when we ran to a store to grab some sunblock, we asked one of the locals for suggestions on where to park. Although this parking lot was perfect, we still had to walk another mile before getting to our corrals.

"How many miles do we have to go before the actual 6.2 miles for the race?" Tracy asked.

"Close to a mile. It's good for you!" I smiled.

"Right!"

The three of them separated from us since they were in their own corral, so David and I kept walking closer to ours. We were in separate corrals since he was grouped in with the runners who would complete it in less than one hour, and I knew that wasn't in the cards for me.

"Good luck, I'll see you at the stage after we finish!" I said and gave him a kiss.

I remember meeting up with my mom at the stage when we did the races years ago since it's an easy landmark to find. All five of us were going at different paces and randomly searching for each other in a sea of 30,000 people would be like a massive game of "Where's Waldo?" except it's full of runners wearing similar brightly colored outfits. This time, we had a specific meeting spot *and* our precious smartphones. The air was crisp and perfect for running as I stood in my corral, surrounded by thousands of runners buzzing with excitement. Just then, a realization hit me.

I need to pee.

Do that now before you start running!

I slipped out of the corral and found the nearest port-o-potty line, which was packed as expected. Thankfully, there were many potties, so the line moved forward faster than I anticipated. I always try not to look into the toilet when I step inside those things, but it's almost impossible to avoid. My nose wrinkled when I looked down and decided to hover over the seat. It had become easier to hold a squat, and I appreciated the strength of my quads at that very moment. It was almost time for the race to start, so I hustled back to my spot.

As the race began, the crowd surged forward, and you could hear the rhythmic pounding of feet hitting the pavement. The first two miles wound through the streets of Mount Pleasant, passing Patriot's Point shortly before reaching the Arthur Ravenel Jr. Bridge, a cable-stayed bridge that offers breathtaking views of Charleston Harbor and the city's historic skyline. I found my pace, feeling strong and steady, but knew the bridge was the biggest challenge ahead. Not even a mile in, I felt like I had to pee again.

Are you kidding me? There's nowhere to stop, and I just used the bathroom!

It might all be in your head since it's a longer route with no pit stops. Don't focus on that and concentrate on the run.

I shifted my thoughts and did everything I could to avoid thinking about waterfalls and toilets. It helped. When I approached the base of the bridge, it loomed ahead like a massive mountain, and I gasped as I stared at the incline. I could feel the strain in my legs as the road began to rise, and the steady hum of footsteps around me slowed slightly as runners pushed through the climb. Not even a tenth of a mile into the incline, I slowed to a walk.

Don't destroy your body on this incline, you're not prepared for something this intense.

I happily obliged what my inner voice said and noticed most people around me had also slowed to a walk. I knew this was the only incline, so I took my time and focused on making it up the concrete mountain in front of me while taking in the scenery. The views from the bridge were beautiful. I could see Charleston's Harbor glittering below, boats scattered throughout the water (both large and small), and downtown Charleston stretching out in the distance. The bridge itself spans 2.5 miles of the race and is the highlight of the event.

You're likely to encounter wind on a normal day by the coast, but this day was exceptionally windy. And with all those people running, you could feel the gentle swaying of the bridge. The feeling was both strange and mesmerizing, like being rocked on a boat, yet still grounded by the solid structure beneath my feet. It would have freaked me out more if I had never experienced this, but on the new bridge, the swaying wasn't as intense as the old bridge. I shuddered at the thought of this many people running on the old bridge.

What if this thing collapses?
Don't create something to worry about.

As I approached the top of the incline, I let out a huge sigh of relief as it shifted into being level, and then started moving down.

"YAY!!" I cried as I picked up speed to run again.

Others around me laughed at my excitement as they shifted as well, and I heard more people behind me letting out cheers as they noticed the change. The decline on the bridge was a huge breath of fresh air, and I thoroughly enjoyed the run on the way down. Although I knew that running on a decline for too long would destroy your quads and toes, this was short-lived like the incline, and I made my way down the bridge. The hardest part of the race was behind me, but I still had to push through for a little under two miles. Running through downtown Charleston was a thrilling and scenic experience, with crowds of people lining the sidewalks. They were holding signs, clapping, and shouting words of encouragement. We passed a fitness facility with a group of women outside doing a spin class, with their stationary bikes facing the street from the sidewalk and cheering for the runners as we ran by. During the last mile, I felt my legs starting to fatigue.

Whew, I'm getting tired.

You are so close! Don't slow down now!

Okay, I've got this.

When I looked at my watch and saw that I had less than half a mile to go, I buckled down to focus and increased my speed. I knew it wouldn't be a personal record since I walked almost a mile during the incline, but I didn't care.

Today's time doesn't matter, you're here for the experience. This race is phenomenal.

When I saw the finish line ahead, I became elated. However, this time it would be physically impossible to break into a full sprint like I did as a teenager. Not because I couldn't do it physically, but because it would have been like a game of pinball trying to avoid bumping into the people around me since we were all packed there together with little space around us for movement. I moved along with the flow of traffic. As I crossed the finish line, I could hear the cheers from people lining the streets holding up encouraging and funny signs, and I smiled. I was in better shape for this race at the age of 42 than I was at 19; something I thought was unattainable.

See what happens when you challenge yourself and continue to persevere?

I wasted so many years giving up too easily.

You can't change the past. Focus on the present for a better future.

Here's to a future with more promise, fulfillment, and success by pushing through the hard parts. The finish line is worth the struggle to get there.

After walking with my fellow sardines, I made my way toward the stage to find David. He probably had enough time to get hydrated, eat food, and write a novel before I finished.

"HEY!" he called out and waved when I got close to the stage.

"How'd you do?"

"That *incline*!!" he said with exasperation. "I was not prepared for that, but I ran it anyway and should have walked instead to have gotten a faster time. I flew down the decline."

"Well, you were faster than me!"

"Comparison is the thief of all joy," he smiled.

"Yeah, I know."

After we all found each other, we gathered at the front to watch the award ceremonies. I stared at them in awe and gawked at their finishing times.

"How did she finish a 10k in only 31 minutes?!" I cried to Tracy, sitting next to me. Deep down, I knew the answer.

They're immortal creatures...centaurs.

No, they're humans just like everyone else out here. They have failed many times, but they didn't give up and kept working hard.

We gathered together and made our way to the shuttle buses. Depending on where you stay in the Charleston area for the race determines whether or not you need to ride a shuttle. If you're staying downtown close to the finish line, you could presumably walk back to your hotel as long as your legs allow you to. If not, you ride a shuttle. As we followed thousands of other people looking for their shuttles, my anxiety reared its ugly head as I stared at the line in front of us that was over two blocks long.

"Oh no...it'll take us *hours* to get back!" I cried.

"There is no way all of these people are going back to Mount Pleasant, let's look around," David said.

"They sent the info of where our shuttle was, did y'all see that on the email? I totally forgot."

"Nope, I didn't even look at the email," both Michael and David replied.

"It said exactly where our pickup would be located, I should have remembered it. I'll just ask someone over here."

"We can find it; we don't need to ask someone!" David protested.

My husband and I are not usually the stereotypical male and female types, but in the case of asking for directions; we are.

"That makes *no* sense to wander around when I can find out where to go right now!" I huffed as I walked over to someone directing the mob of people.

"Hi! We're looking for the shuttle to get back to Mount Pleasant, is this the line here?"

"No, you need the one that's three blocks ahead and take a right."

We followed his directions to our shuttle and discovered there was no line for ours. We climbed on the bus immediately and picked our seats in the back.

"See how much faster we found the correct location just by asking a *stranger*? So crazy!" I teased.

"Uh-huh," he smiled, "Thank you."

"David, I thought you would run back over the bridge instead of riding the bus!" Michael said.

"I would have no problem doing that," he laughed.

"I would!" I said and stared out the window as the bus pulled away.

I was convinced that every bus from every school district in the Southeastern United States was in downtown Charleston at that moment. We enjoyed the ride back across the bridge, taking in the view from a different perspective than the way we crossed it not long before. Although the logistics of participating in this race were more involved than local races, the effort was well worth the experience. Zack ended up with a time of just over an hour and had never run farther than 2 miles before the race. He had no idea how much youth was on his side in so many ways.

I once saw a quote that said, "Youth is wasted on the young," and I could not agree more, which is why I will continue to stay active until I no longer can.

We will definitely do this race again.

Our family event and the incline.

-20-

ELATION AND HEARTBREAK

Skibner and I decided to do another She-Tris event together at I'On subdivision in Mount Pleasant. She was doing the Triathlon again, and I signed up for the Duathlon, which is a run-bike-run. I had been curious about this type of multi-sport race and wanted to see how I liked it. My portion was to run 1 mile, bike 9 miles, then run 2 more miles. For me, the time of completing this distance was similar to running a 10k race. Even though it's a sprint distance, it still takes endurance to keep a strong, steady pace for an hour.

Leading up to the race I was excited, but the nervousness started creeping in a few days before. I knew the Duathlon distance for these events didn't have as many people as the Triathlon but was interested in experiencing it. Although I was more focused on competing against my own times, my natural competitiveness kicked in on occasion. Being mediocre on the spectrum of speed, standing on the podium had only been a pipedream that seemed so far-fetched it would be many years before I could experience it; if it were *ever* possible.

I slept well, only waking up once. The problem was that I woke up at a time that was questionable whether or not I should eat breakfast or do the race fasted. If I ate too soon before the race, I might have cramped up. If I didn't eat, I risked the chance of running out of fuel. My body wasn't used to consistently training while fasted. It was right on the line, and I decided to skip out on breakfast.

Let's see how this goes; you've done some fasted workouts before. If you crash, you'll learn from it. Trial and error will help you determine your limits.

FIRST RUN (1 mile)

Five of us lined up for the Duathlon portion of the race, ranging in age from early thirties to early fifties, and I was the second oldest in the group. Although I had learned that you can't judge a book by its cover, I looked at the other ladies with me. There was no telling which of us was the fastest just by appearance.

You're not out here to win, you're here because you love doing this.

This is very true, but I also would prefer not to come in last place if at all possible.

It was a casual start with a handful of us, so there wasn't even a horn; just a verbal "GO!" that set us off on our first run. The start and finish took place in a parking lot, then went down a shaded trail. We were all jogging together, and I was at the back of the pack when we passed a couple on the path. The wife was cheering for us, and I heard a familiar voice. Then, I saw her face.

"Rhi-Rhi!!!" I cried when I saw her.

"OH! That's my cousin! Go Erin, you've got this!!" she squealed excitedly and jumped up and down as I stopped to hug her before running off. She lived in the Charleston area, but it slipped my mind to let her know

I was doing the event since we would only be there for less than 24 hours. Her husband started competing in local triathlons in the area a couple of years prior, but he got serious with his races quickly and became a beast in the triathlon community. He started placing in the top three of his age group in most local triathlons that he competes in, and they travel for some destination races.

We continued our run at a steady pace, and we all slightly spread out before we made it back to the transition area. I strapped on my helmet, hopped on my bike, and headed out for the course.

Wow, that was a quick run and I loved that as a warmup!

THE BIKE (9 miles)

We took off on our bikes and hopped on the course with people directing us along the route. As we approached a turn, a volunteer stood on the corner and instructed us to slow down.

"She's telling us to slow down at a *race!*" I laughed after we passed.

"It's for our *safety!*" huffed a woman next to me.

"I know, it was a *joke!*"

She shook her head at me.

Don't worry about Karen; you could be the female version of Kevin Hart, and she won't laugh at your jokes right now because you are racing. You're not everyone's cup of tea, and that's okay.

That is *definitely* the truth, and I have learned to accept it. I'm outspoken, passionate, nutty, easily excited, and can sometimes be a little much for some people. My sense of humor is warped, and I'm not afraid to speak my mind (even if it ruffles a few feathers), but I thrive in authenticity, honesty, and mutual respect. Not everyone is going to like me, but those who do appreciate me for who I am...a goofball who will cheer louder for other people than I will for myself.

The bike ride was consistent, I went back and forth passing and getting passed by several of the same people. We were mixed in with the ladies doing the Triathlon portion, so we all blended together. It was like a game of tag, they would get bursts of energy, then mine would come in, and so forth. Like the previous triathlons, the bike ride was enjoyable, and I felt like a kid again riding through the neighborhood. At the end of the ride, a big burst of energy surged through my body and kicked into high speed until I had to dismount my bike and run to the transition area. I threw off my helmet, grabbed a swig of water, and did a jog/wobble on my noodle legs to head out for the run.

SECOND RUN (2 miles)

The directions were much clearer the second time around with the run since it started out the same. Only this time, I was alone because we had all spread out along the route. At this point, I was second-guessing my choice to skip breakfast. The sweet spot for me with training while fasting is to keep the workouts under one hour as long as it's first thing in the morning. It was almost one hour of pushing harder than I was used to, and I was starting to feel it.

Should I have eaten a small breakfast instead of skipping out?

The only thing you can do right now is focus on what's in front of you. Get through this and make a mental note of the learning experience.

I was less than half a mile in, and fortunately, it was a quick out-and-back route where we turned around at the one-mile point. Our group doing the duathlon had all gotten spread out on the course, so I had no idea where we all were with each other. It was actually a relief to not know, since I couldn't worry about it.

Okay. I can do this. Dang, this is really tough, I don't have much fuel left in my tank. This is not an easy run like it was in the last triathlon.

You cannot change the past, focus on what's in front of you.

When it comes to endurance races, it's more of a mind game than a physical game. Of course, you need physical training, but if your mind isn't in the right place it will greatly affect how well you do. Our minds can hold us back or propel us forward with the right perspective, which is how it is with most things in life. I saw the halfway point ahead and felt a sigh of relief run through my body.

Holy cow, I am running on fumes. How am I going to make it through this?

Look at that, you're halfway through. Only one mile left to go!

I saw Karen from the bike ride coming up that was close behind me, and we were getting ready to pass each other. She looked like she was in the zone.

I smiled at her and cheered, "Great job, we're almost finished!"

Her icy glare could have frozen me in a glacier that rested a mile beneath the Arctic Ocean.

Yikes.

Don't worry about her, she's doing her own thing. Focus on yours and finish.

It was less than half a mile to go, and the fumes I was running on had turned into tiny, sporadic puffs of air. I was completely spent.

Please let me get to the finish line without passing out. Please...

You've got this, you're almost there...

The directions to the finish line rounded a different corner, so I wasn't exactly sure how far away I was until I made the final turn. It was like a shining beacon of light had come out of the clouds when I saw the finish line about 75 yards in front of me. A wave of adrenaline came rushing through my veins, my vision narrowed at the finish line, and I took off as fast as I could. A smile spread across my face, I ran through the finish line and gave high-fives to some little hands that were reaching out for me.

YOU DID IT!!

YES! FINALLY!! Now, I can EAT!!

I grabbed a bottle of water and headed back to the transition area to get a granola bar and protein shake out of my bag. My hunger pangs weren't as strong, since the adrenaline was quite a big distractor, and I felt fine but also knew I needed to refuel. After I ate, I walked around looking for my cousin. She and her husband were standing with a few other ladies they knew who had competed, and we squealed again when we saw each other.

"How did you do?" she asked excitedly.

"I'm not sure; I *think* I was in the top three, but don't want to get my hopes up. That would be *so* cool though, I have never stood on a podium!"

We split up so I could wait for Skibner to cross the finish line for the triathlon. The music was blaring, people were cheering, and there were vendors everywhere. I kept trying to pull up the results, but my phone was acting wonky. Suddenly, Rhi ran up to me.

"YOU GOT FIRST PLACE!!!" she screamed.

"ARE YOU SERIOUS?!?!"

She showed me the results on her phone, and we jumped up and down together squealing like a couple of teenage girls and hugged. Several people around us chuckled at our overdramatic behavior, but we didn't care, we matched each other's energy. Actually, she has *more* energy than I do. The feeling was a level of excitement I had never experienced, on top of the accomplishment of finishing the race.

I couldn't wait to call my family and tell them the news. David and the kids were super excited and said they wished they had been there with me. My mom was surprised and happy, and Skibner cheered loudly. The floating I felt on Cloud Nine was short-lived and shattered into a million pieces after talking to Michael. After trying to reach him earlier, I had been somewhat hesitant to call him since he can be pessimistic at times.

"I got first place!" I exclaimed into the phone.

"In your age group?"

"No! Overall!"

"For..."

"The *Duathlon* I just did!!"

"I'm confused..."

"Well, there were only five people that did this part of the event-"

He cut me off and started laughing hysterically.

"Even if this is the *only* time in my life I get to stand on a podium, I'll take it!" I cried, defensively.

"So, you got first place in an event where there were more people who *were* on the podium than who *weren't* on it? That's hilarious."

All the excitement that exploded quickly went down the toilet, and Skibner saw the look of heartbreak on my face.

"What did he say?" she asked.

"He's laughing at me because there were only a handful of people who participated in this event."

"WHAT?? Tell him to SHUT UP!!" she cried.

I relayed the message, and he laughed again.

"Whatever. You're stupid," I said half-jokingly and hung up.

It felt like I had just gotten punched in the gut, feeling deeply hurt and confused. I was excited and proud of my achievement, but his words cut through my joy, making it feel small and insignificant. I couldn't help but wonder if I had overreacted about winning first place, doubting myself. It was a sharp sting of betrayal because I expected support and validation from the people who loved me, and wished he could see how much it meant for me to experience something like this, especially coming from where I started.

Why wouldn't he be excited for his sister? He knows I just started doing this a year ago! Why didn't he show me support and positive encouragement?

When someone belittles other people's accomplishments, it's not you, it's them. They are projecting their insecurities onto you.
He was so encouraging when we were kids. Why is he the opposite now as an adult?
That's on him, not you. He doesn't see the mindset that you have now and doesn't know how much you have grown.
I roamed around aimlessly, waiting for the awards ceremony. It was a constant wave of emotions between extreme happiness and devastation. One minute I was elated, the next minute I was heartbroken. If this had come from a stranger, I could have brushed it off; but not when it came from someone who had such an important role in my life. Robbie mirrors my excitement when it comes to accomplishments and is a wonderful cheerleader. I love both of my brothers immensely, and their opinions hold a lot of weight in my life, but there are also times when boundaries need to be set when there is a lack of support.
The worst thing you can do is let one person ruin this. You worked so hard, enjoy every second of it!
I pushed the negative thoughts aside and waited to be called to stand on the podium. The excitement was overwhelming, and I still couldn't believe it.
I don't care if this is the only time I ever get to stand on a podium, this is incredible!
The struggle was worth it!
After I walked over to the gift table for the top winners in each group and picked out some sunglasses, Karen walked up to me.

"Congratulations!" she said with a smile and hugged me.

"Thank you!" I exclaimed and hugged her back.

I guess Karen isn't really a Karen after all.

Yep, she was just focused on her journey.

A few days later, I called Tracy and told her about my phone call with her husband. Michael had no idea I was so upset, and Tracy didn't even know about our conversation. After I told her what happened, she fussed at him for being oblivious and unsupportive. The next day, he called me.

"I didn't realize this was such a big deal for you, I didn't mean to upset you," he said, solemnly.

"I don't think you realize how much your opinion and support mean to me."

"I'm flattered, but sometimes I wish you wouldn't listen to me when I say something stupid like that."

"You peed all over my cornflakes. They were drowning."

He laughed, "I know, and I'm sorry. I think it's great you're doing all of this, and I'm impressed with how far you have come. Honestly, I'm a little jealous."

There is the projection.

I paused for a few seconds, shocked.

"Well then, start training and come to the next event wearing a wig," I teased.

"Don't tempt me!"

"But seriously, if I can do this, so can you."

"Maybe."

"You don't know if you don't try. I think you could do more than you realize, you just have to *want* to make the effort for it."

The road bike makes a huge difference!

It is physically impossible for me to avoid giving fives.

-21-

GO BIG OR GO HOME

"How did you do on your last 5k?" my chiropractor asked when I went in for an adjustment.

"Great! It was a personal best time of 30:16!"

"That's awesome!" he cheered.

"My goal this year is to get my 5k time under 30 minutes, and I was *so* close! Hopefully I can do it in the next race."

"When is your next race?"

"This weekend."

He shook his head. "No, that's too big of a jump to improve your time so soon."

"It's only an improvement of 17 seconds."

"I don't think you realize how big of a gap that is," he replied.

"For a 5k? It can't hurt to try."

"Yeah, that's true. Good luck!"

I smiled.

Has he bumped his head?

I was torn between having thoughts of self-doubt and retaliation by saying, "Watch me, bro." He's not particularly a huge fan of running.

Don't let this deter you from trying to achieve your goal.

I'm not. I'm stubborn, and although he likely meant well, he challenged me without realizing it.

The fire under my butt was officially ignited. Leading up to the Run Hard Community event that Saturday, the odds weren't in my favor. After we went out to eat the night before the race, my stomach was in horrific pain, and it still felt weak in the morning. I didn't sleep well, and where I was in my menstrual cycle was the worst place to be for running a race. The weather was also 48 degrees and raining. I was so fired up about the conversation a few days earlier that I was on edge. My goal was set, and I was at least going to *try*.

We prepared for the weather that morning, and David duct-taped our shoes. This worked out better for his shoes since my only pairs of running shoes were mesh, and there was no good preparation running in the rain with mesh shoes. He found a pack of ponchos he had ordered earlier in the year when we thought there would be rain for a race, so he threw those in the car.

He was doing the Half-Marathon again and had his own goal, and I had my goal of reaching a time under 30 minutes for the 5k. He knew I was way more stressed than I should have been.

"You have a lot going against you today. You can hit your goal, but don't beat yourself up if you don't get it *today*. You can do it in another race if you don't get it, just do what you can," he said to me in the car on the way to the race.

Reason #548,971 why this man continues to be my favorite person.

We looked super stylish with our ponchos and taped-up shoes. I didn't care, I was already miserably cold in the weather. As we walked to the starting area, the duct tape immediately started peeling off my shoes.

"Ugh, great!"

"Oh no!" he said as he saw me tugging at the pieces flapping from my shoes.

"I do not want to deal with trying to pull these off while running, so I might as well suck it up and run with wet feet," I said and ripped them off.

I had been an assistant coach with the Run Hard group at Alex's school for the past month, so I knew several people involved with the program. Coach Jesse organizes all of the Run Hard events and lined everyone up at the start line. His kids also go to Alex's school, and I told him earlier in the week about my goal.

When I lined up, he smiled and told me, "If you hit 30:01, I'm sending you home!"

"If I hit 30:01 I'm sending *myself* home!!" I said and laughed.

I was at the front of the line off to the side when the horn blew and took off. The poncho kept my body dry, but my hands were wet and freezing. Almost immediately, water sank into my shoes, so my feet quickly became wet and freezing as well. Starting the race, I knew this was not my day. My legs felt weak. My left heel hurt; my right Achilles tendon hurt. After a few minutes, the pain subsided until my *side* started to hurt. It was the hardest, most miserable 5k I had experienced since I started running the previous year.

This. Really. Sucks.

I periodically looked at my watch to see how I was doing at my pace. At mile 2, I stopped looking because it didn't seem like I would be able to hit my goal that day, so my inner voice took over.

Stop looking at your watch and just GO.

That last mile felt brutal, but I kept pushing through. In the last few races, I had been able to kick into a sprint the last 100 meters, but it took everything I had to pick up the pace just a little bit for the last 50 meters to cross the finish line. I had NO idea if my time had hit that goal of being under 30 minutes, so I waited for the results. When they were ready, I eagerly went online preparing for the possibility of it being just over, but then I saw it...

29:56

"Oh my gosh!!! I DID IT!!" I squealed to a friend next to me and jumped up and down like a little girl.

Next to the time was my age division place; FIRST PLACE. I almost fell over from shock. This was a bonus, because the fastest runners were either doing the 10k or Half Marathon, and I had *never* placed first in a 5k because the odds were so low with my mediocre speed. With the weather being lousy, more people also dropped out at the last minute. I didn't care, I soaked it all in because the suffering to cross the finish line was worth every bit of effort. It had become *SO* much more than just running...it was all about a complete shift of mindset that I didn't ever want to go back to the old me or the old inner voice. The old me is gone. She taught me a lot about who I want to be for the rest of my life, and I couldn't wait to see what the future held. I wanted to step outside my comfort zone even more. Running started the snowball effect, and the snowball continued to grow in front of my eyes.

Don't ever let someone else's negativity hold you back from achieving your goals.

The prize for winning the top three in each age group was a Christmas ornament, which I will forever display on our Christmas tree.

-22-

RECONNECTING

In 2023, we started a family tradition for our birthdays. When David asked for birthday gift ideas, I told him that I wanted to take a weekend trip to somewhere along the coast that we had never been; and I asked for the location to be a surprise. The specifications were to be somewhere within driving distance, brand new to us, and on the coast. I was very clear about not wanting to know where we were going, and he kept it from the kids so they wouldn't accidentally slip up and ruin the surprise. His biggest mistake was telling his sweet mom. He had planned a trip to Tybee Island, Georgia, for the weekend and told her about the surprise location.

While Mimi was over for a visit a couple of weeks before we left, we were sitting in the living room when she asked David, "Did you get that list of things I sent you to do in Tybee?"

He shot her a glare that was powerful enough to reverse the earth's rotation, and she immediately realized what she had done. I didn't respond to what she said, just continued to focus on what I was reading; but it was too late, I already knew the surprise location for my birthday weekend.

"So, do you know where we're going?" David asked curiously the day before we left.

I have an *extremely* hard time not being honest, especially to my favorite person in the world.

I smiled sheepishly, "Yep."

"Was it that day my mom said something?"

"Yep."

"Ugh, I *knew* it!!"

"It's not a big deal, I had it narrowed down to there and one other place. Plus, I would have figured it out once we got on the road and you had to plug the address into the GPS. It's all good, I'm just excited to go somewhere new!"

Tybee Island is a barrier island located off the coast of Georgia, about 20 minutes from Savannah. It is a busy town with a beautiful beach boardwalk full of shopping, restaurants, and my favorite part was the pier. It reminded me of a smaller scale of Myrtle Beach. The next morning, we sat in the condo enjoying our coffee, muffins, and an ocean view of the cargo ships headed for the Savannah Port. The breeze, the smell, and the sound of the ocean have always made me feel at home, regardless of the town we are visiting.

"Would you want to explore Daufuskie Island? There's a ferry leaving from Savannah that we could take over there," David asked, looking up from his laptop.

"Oh, Daufuskie Island! We have always wanted to go there!"

"I know, that's why I'm asking!"

"Yes, let's do it!" I exclaimed.

"Okay, we need to walk out the door in 15 minutes to make it to the ferry."

I stared at him like a deer in headlights.

Oh no. We're still in our pajamas.

We went into Ludicrous Speed Mode and ran around like wild monkeys getting ready as quickly as possible, especially with two kids who weren't in a super big rush to get out the door. I'm convinced they don't understand what it means to hustle unless they're going to a waterpark, a friend's house, or there's a spider in the room. After we rented a golf cart and spent the day exploring Daufuskie, we were mesmerized and in love with the island. David booked another weekend trip a couple of months later to spend a long weekend exploring more of what it had to offer.

Daufuskie Island is a unique place. It's located between Hilton Head, South Carolina, and Savannah, Georgia, that is only accessible by boat. The island is quite remote, with a couple of small general stores with limited groceries and other necessities that you might find in a gas station, and the only cars on the island are owned by the locals. There are a few small restaurants, a cute little coffee shop in the old schoolhouse, a farmers market with local fruits and vegetables grown on the island, a distillery, a vineyard, and several gift shops. With its unspoiled nature, diverse wildlife, and laid-back atmosphere, Daufuskie Island is a peaceful escape from the hustle and bustle of modern life. The main mode of transportation around the island is by golf carts, and we *love* riding around on golf carts. Well, we love golf carts when it's warm and sunny outside, let me specify this before I go into details of the race that takes place in the middle of January.

David had been talking and obsessing about the island ever since we took those two trips, so it came as no surprise when I was searching for races and came across something I knew he would be interested in.

"Do you want to do the Daufuskie Island Half-Marathon in January?"

"YES!!!" he cried immediately, without hesitation.

Being such a reserved introvert, it's a huge deal for him to be *so* excited about any race. I laughed at his reaction and got us registered.

A race in January. That is going to be COLD. Didn't we just do a race in the cold rain?

As much fun as running a race in the cold rain sounds (it's not), we have to consider it for these events when traveling out of town for a destination race.

Put on your big-girl panties, it'll be fine.

We planned for the kids to stay with grandparents while we took our weekend trip, and they complained about not going with us. I couldn't imagine they would have too much fun, waiting a couple of hours in the cold for us to finish running. When I discovered that Kaitlyn's first school dance competition was the same weekend we were going out of town, we had already paid for the race, ferry tickets, and accommodations. I felt *extremely* guilty about leaving.

"Mom, you come to every event I have, and there will be several more. It's okay!" she said when I apologized to her that we would be missing it.

"I know, but..."

"Mom! It's okay!"

A mother's guilt for missing important events in her child's life is an emotional and overwhelming experience. For many parents, the pressure to balance work, personal obligations, and family can lead to moments where we have to make difficult choices. Even though Grammy was taking her, and everything was set, I still felt intense guilt over missing it.

Maybe we should cancel our trip.

NO! Like she said, you go to every event, and she knows that. She knows she can count on you, and you have someone she loves and trusts to be there with her. You and David must take this time together. Your family started with the two of you, and it will end with the two of you. The kids will grow up knowing and seeing how much their mom and dad love each other and spend time together. It's a crucial part of nurturing your marriage and your family.

The weekend arrived, and we drove to Hilton Head to catch the ferry over to Daufuskie. I did the driving so he could do some work on his laptop. I had discovered that when we're traveling out of town, he's more on edge driving to our destination than when he's distracted with work while riding in the passenger seat. I'm more patient behind the wheel and able to multi-task by following the GPS and driving, so this is the usual way we travel. Coming home, he's more relaxed and ready to drive without the other "horrible" drivers on the road annoying the complete mess out of him.

How ironic that we're spending a kid-free getaway weekend together during my least favorite week of the month. The joys of womanhood.

There's nothing you can do about that, Sweet Pea. It is what it is.

We arrived at the Haig Point Embarkation in Hilton Head to pick up our race packets, then headed over to our ferry dock a few minutes down the road. We loaded up our luggage and settled on the ferry, along with other runners there for the race.

We're surrounded by centaurs!

I struck up a conversation with a couple sitting close to us when I heard them talking about other marathons they had completed over the years. Kelley and Joe were from Charleston, and one of their favorite activities to do together is to travel for destination races...specifically marathons.

"Have y'all done the Boston Marathon?"

"Oh yes, several times. We love it!"

I looked at David, "One day? Maybe?"

"You know it," he said with a smile.

"We don't even care about our times anymore; we just do these races for the experience. We enjoy traveling and running them together," Kelley said with an infectious smile.

"I hope to be able to run with him one day," I said.

"You will!" David chimed in.

When we arrived at Daufuskie Island after our ferry ride, we hopped in a transport van with a few other runners to be dropped off at the condo we were staying in. I overheard one lady talking to another about her training schedule.

"I do a 10-mile long run each week, so I'm conditioned well to do a Half-Marathon whenever they pop up in a different location I'd like to travel to. I love destination races!"

These are my people. I want to be like them when I grow up.

You grow up a little bit more every single day.

Our shuttle dropped us off at the Sandy Lane Condos, close to Bloody Point. We rode around this area during our previous visits and were excited to stay on a different part of the island since we stayed in Melrose before. We took our luggage up to the condo, let ourselves in, and gawked over our home for the next two days. It was a beautifully decorated corner condo that had views of the ocean from the front and the side. When David originally booked the condo, he anticipated the kids and Mimi would come with us, but those plans didn't work out with Kaitlyn's dance competition. So, there we were; just the two of us in a three-bedroom condo. My natural inclination was to invite someone, *anyone*, to join us. This is where our differences clash.

Maybe one day we can become close with other runners and take group trips together. Maybe I can even find girl groups to do destination races with!

We settled in for the evening, prepared the food we brought for dinner, and watched some shows together before heading off to bed early. When I woke up the next morning, I felt rested and relaxed. For some reason, I didn't have any race nerves even though this was my second Half-Marathon. The time limit for this race was twice as long as the one in Myrtle Beach, so I didn't feel any pressure. Plus, the laid-back atmosphere on the island was contagious. Since the race didn't start until 9:30 am and we woke up at 6:00, we took our time settling into the morning with our coffee and muffins while watching the sunrise over the ocean.

I save muffins for the weekend to enjoy with my coffee as a special treat. There's a simple, comforting joy in sitting down with a fluffy muffin and a hot cup of coffee. As you take the first sip, the aroma and flavors of coffee awaken your senses, perfectly complementing the soft bite of the muffin. The contrast between the moist crumb and the coffee's smooth bitterness creates the perfect balance. It's my favorite morning indulgence, with a Pumpkin Cinnamon Roll muffin as my preferred flavor. It was a delightful start to the morning before the self-inflicted torture of our legs by running 13.1 miles.

"I'm going to run with you today," he told me.

"What? Really? You don't have to do that."

"I know I don't have to; I *want* to."

"Are you sure? I know you have a goal you're trying to hit with this distance, and I don't want to hold you back from doing that."

"I'm positive," he said with a smile.

"Okay," I replied and returned the smile.

Looks like I'll get the opportunity to run with him sooner than I expected. I'll take it.

The race start and finish line were in Haig Point on the island, which was the only section we had not explored since it is a private gated community. We bundled up and hopped on our rented golf cart, headed for the start. Riding around on a golf cart at 48 degrees was quite different than the joyrides we took over the hot summer. We parked our cart just as the full marathon started, and we stood to the side watching them run past us. Several men already had their shirts off, but we knew from experience they wouldn't need them for long anyway since the sun was shining bright outside. The course consisted of one 13.1-mile loop, so the full marathon racers completed the loop twice. In previous years, there was a 3-loop option for the extra-crazy centaurs who wanted to run an ultramarathon, but it had been reduced to a half and full.

"Could you imagine running 39.3 miles?" I asked.

"Not anytime soon!" he replied.

We dropped our bags at a station with our names and bib numbers to keep until after we were done with the race, then walked over to a large, heated tent area where all the runners were gathered. There was a buffet of food available, with fruit, cinnamon rolls, and coffee. The smell was intoxicating between the coffee and rolls.

"I'm going to have some more coffee. Do you want some?" he asked.

"Not unless I want to stop an extra three times during the race to pee."

"No coffee for you!" he laughed.

Although the heated tent was warmer than outside, it was still cold. I couldn't tell if my shivers were from the weather or the race nerves, although I assumed 90% was from the weather since I wasn't nervous. I was looking forward to running with him.

"Are you sure you're okay with running at a geriatric speed today?"

He laughed, "Yes, we'll be old together!"

"I'm the tortoise and you're the hare!"

After the race director made the last announcements, everyone made their way out of the tent and over to the start line. The number of people running the Half-Marathon was about double the number running the full. With no outside cars allowed on the island, runners are surrounded by natural beauty and a serene atmosphere, making it an ideal setting for those seeking a peaceful yet challenging race. Since there were no main roads to close for traffic, the time limit was twice as long as it was in Myrtle Beach, allowing even more people the opportunity to try a distance they never thought was possible. It is also relatively flat, with a varied terrain of pavement, gravel, dirt, and shaded paths lined with moss-draped oak trees. The route allows runners to enjoy the surroundings and the race itself without the safety distractions of heavy traffic.

The energy grew quickly as we waited at the start line, with upbeat music pumping, people jumping up and down, cheering, and warming up for a race they were about to start stripping their clothes off for. After the National Anthem played, the countdown began, and the horn blew. I watched the timer begin as we ran under the start line with the crowd of people, our feet pounding the pavement together. We were both wearing light jackets over our shirts and stuffed them into our running packs about a mile into the run.

That didn't take long.

Haig Point spans over 1,000 acres of preserved nature, and we enjoyed the scenery as we ran down winding paved trails that lead through ancient oak trees draped in Spanish moss. One of the community's main features is a 29-hole golf course with spectacular views of the water and lush surroundings. The first 2 miles of the course went through the main entrance of the community, so we were able to see another section of the island and gaped at its beauty.

As we exited the entrance, we passed by the only pit stop along the course, with a couple of port-o-potties, water station, and snacks.

"You don't need to go now, do you?" he asked.

"Not yet," I laughed.

This man really knows me and my bladder.

We took a right and headed down the road, keeping a steady pace as we ran together, chatting along the way, and discussing how beautiful it was to see the island from a different perspective. The fact that we were talking while running meant that we weren't over-exerting ourselves, and I was thrilled to run with him. Although I normally talked to myself during races, it was nice to talk to someone *outside* my head.

"This is so nice!" I exclaimed.

"It really is! I enjoy running together!"

"If at any time you want to speed up, you can go. I know you're not used to running this slowly."

"No, I'm good. I'm happy to stay with you."

I smiled as we continued along the course. At the 5-mile marker, I looked at my watch and noticed we had been running for an hour.

"If we keep it up at this pace, I'll shatter my last Half-Marathon time!"

"What did you get last time?"

"It took me 3 hours and almost 16 minutes."

"Oh yeah, we'll beat that for sure."

"Don't jinx it!"

At mile 7, I realized I hadn't eaten anything yet when my stomach suddenly screamed for food, so we slowed down to a walk for a couple of minutes to eat a Picky Bar. He ate one of his Gu gels, which worked well for him. Since I wasn't used to eating much refined sugar, I had spent the previous months experimenting with healthier options, including Huma gels.

"Are you ready to pick it back up?"

"Give me 30 seconds," I said and took a sip of water from the bottle I was carrying. "Okay, let's go."

We picked up the pace and kept a steady run again, and I noticed that running with him had significantly increased my overall pace. I wasn't sure if this was a good thing or bad thing at the time, considering this was a longer distance, and didn't want to burn out before reaching the finish. Only 2 ½ miles later, I had to slow down to a short walk again and take in a Huma gel.

"You okay?" he asked.

"Yeah, I think I'm running out of gas."

"We only have a little over 3 miles to go!"

"Once we get to the 10-mile marker, I'll speed up again. I need a minute here."

"You can do it! Let's go *now*!"

"Not yet."

"Come on, let's go!"

"David, *NO*. Just let me get to mile 10 and I will start running again," I stood firm, listening to my body and knowing we were on different levels.

We spent the next five minutes walking, and I could tell he was getting anxious to run again. Bless his impatient, natural endurance, immortal heart.

"I need to listen to my song," I said, pulling it up on my phone and scrolling to *Born For This* by The Score. I immersed myself in the words, and let my mind and heart go as the motivation soared. Music takes me places mentally and emotionally unlike anything else.

"Look, there's mile marker 10 up ahead! Let's go!"

"We only have a 5k to run!" I said and smiled at the realization of how far we had gone.

I noticed that since we started running 5k races, our mindsets shifted. A 5k used to be a big deal to me, but it had transformed into just being a somewhat simple race. "Oh, it's just a 5k," had become a normal response like I was walking to the mailbox.

That distance still wasn't simple (especially when I pushed it), but the rest of my day was normal like nothing happened. There was no need for extra rest or recovery, it had just become a morning workout.

What am I turning into?
A centaur.
Yeah, right. I wish!

We picked up the pace right at mile 10 to complete a 5k, only this time my legs were anything but feeling fresh. They felt weak and tired. I pushed through the fatigue for the next mile and a half until I saw the opening to the ocean. We ran along a wooden bridge that turned into a beachfront path that went right along the water. My face lit up with pure joy.

This is my happy place.

After I moved away from the coast, it felt like a piece of me was missing. I didn't understand it for years until one day I went out with my brothers for a boat ride on Lake Murray. As I closed my eyes, I felt the breeze in my hair, sunshine on my face, and the sound of the water splashing along the side of the boat, the smell radiating through the air; the realization hit me with an overwhelming force. I finally realized what one simple thing filled my soul.

The water! The water is what I have been missing! It all makes sense now!

Not only had I spent my childhood living near the

ocean, but I also spent it on the Intracoastal Waterway in my parents' riverboat business. As a child, I was on the boats just *because*, and when I was 15, I started working for them, spending a substantial amount of time on the water. One of my favorite jobs was as the first mate, tying the lines on the dock to secure a 365-passenger riverboat using ropes the size of my leg. It was comical to watch a 125-lb. teenage girl wrangle those lines like a pro wrestler, using my body weight to pull the massive boat to the dock and quickly tie it up like an Eagle Scout. My dad and I still joke about how tiny the lines are on his pontoon boat whenever I'm tying or untying it to take a ride on the lake.

"This is gorgeous!" I cried.

"It sure is!"

I had a renewed source of energy as we ran along the beachfront sidewalk, winding through pristine landscaping. I was so mesmerized by the view that I had a hard time focusing on the path in front of me until I saw a photographer ahead.

"Let's do silly pictures!"

"Of course, you want to do silly pictures."

"It makes it more fun and interesting!"

"Uh-huh."

As we came up to the photographer, I heard the clicking of the camera and threw my arms out to the sides, like we were birds. David threw his arms out too, and we all laughed as the photographer took pictures.

We're flying through the course!

Here comes your inner child.

That's right! It's okay to have fun as an adult! In fact, we should all do it!

"I really hope we're close, my legs are getting extremely tired," I said.

"We are, we have less than a mile to go."

Okay, less than a mile. I can do this.

We continued along the path, and I felt myself slowing down, my legs giving in to the fatigue.

Oh no, not now!

"We're so close! *Let's sprint!*" he cheered.

"You have lost your mind! I can't sprint yet!"

We made the turn off the paved beach path, and I took one last look at the water as we moved inland. It started to blur together where we were and how far the finish line was, but I kept pushing. We were *very* close.

"Look, there's the 13-mile marker!" he said.

Oh my gosh. Thank you.

After passing the mile marker, we took a right turn and saw lines of people cheering on the runners as they ran through the finish line.

"Give me your hand!" I shouted.

He grabbed my hand, and we broke into a sprint for the last tenth of a mile. My adrenaline kicked in, and his strong grip held on tightly as we ran like little kids through the finish line. I was running, smiling, laughing, and wheezing all at the same time. It was a perfect blend of multi-tasking.

"We were such dorks running through the finish line holding hands, but I don't care!" I laughed.

"You shouldn't!"

I used to scoff at couples like that, but only because I wanted it for myself. People indeed project their insecurities onto others, and I was guilty of doing it as well until I developed awareness.

After having kids, many marriages face a gradual shift as the focus of daily life becomes centered around the children, and we were not an exception. Time once spent nurturing our relationship shifted into parenting duties, with less room for intimacy and emotional connection. Running together had brought us closer, deepening our relationship on a level I didn't think was possible for us. We truly had become one unit, a team.

Running gave us not only a common goal but also the chance to rediscover each other outside our roles as parents. The joy of accomplishing races strengthened our partnership by trying new adventures together. No relationship is perfect, and we still have our squabbles (especially both of us having strong personalities), but the moments of disagreements had become smaller and less important compared to the fun and connection we had found through the quirks we shared. When one of us goes off into the deep end, the other reels us in, and vice versa. The key has been embracing our imperfections and realizing that even when we're ridiculous, the joy of being together far outweighs any minor arguments.

Although David married a firecracker, my fire had dimmed significantly after adjusting to motherhood. Between the overall exhaustion and desire for calmness and peace, I just didn't want to argue and stopped speaking up for myself and setting boundaries; two things that were imperative for a balanced, healthy relationship and communication between us. I finally realized that I was only hurting myself for not only shoving my priorities down to the bottom of the list, but also not vocalizing those needs to my partner in life. Although I had grown and changed, I still needed to hold on to some of those personality traits that drew us to each other and what we valued. We both respected strength, and that was an important part for us. We also learned when to pick our battles and speak up when it was necessary, not just because a fleeting thought came flying into our emotional heads.

Would you really want him to be able to read your mind?

Um, no. I wouldn't wish for anyone to see how much of a hot mess it is in there.

That's why you should continue speaking up for yourself and setting boundaries. People treat you the way you let them.

"This has been my favorite race out of all the ones we have done," he said with a smile.

"I agree. It was fantastic!"

We were still warm from all the running, so we continued to walk around while I got my medal engraved with my name and time. Although I knew we had completed the race faster than the last one I did, I was not expecting to see a 31-minute improvement and was completely floored.

"Oh my gosh! It was 2:44:37!!"

"Next year it'll be under 2 hours!"

"Did you fall and bump your head?" I teased.

"No, but I know you can do it."

"Maybe one day."

I didn't care much about a faster time in the future, I was focused on how much we enjoyed this race together and looked forward to our future adventures.

Team Courtney; where being dorky is cool.

-23-

AN UNEXPECTED ISSUE

Growing older has presented so many *fun* challenges (insert sarcasm here). Yet, I was completely sidelined by a new and embarrassing health issue that thrust itself into my life with no warning whatsoever. I don't feel women are given enough notice of what interesting surprises can pop up in mid-life.

Alex and I signed up to do the Cupid's Chase 5k in Columbia just before Valentine's Day. David was on call for work and had to skip this one, so it was some good Mother-Son bonding time. Alex is famous for not going to the bathroom and not eating when he's too busy doing *anything* else, so I must remind him regularly. We both used the bathrooms before the race, even though he "claimed" he didn't have to go.

"Uh-huh, I'm sure you don't. Go anyway."

He was at the age where he was almost too old to go into the ladies' restroom, but too young to go into the men's restroom by himself. He hates having to go to the restroom with me, but luckily for him, they had port-o-potties set up for the race and he was able to avoid such embarrassment as going into the ladies' restroom with his mom. Poor little guy.

We strolled around the park checking out some vendors and other people set up with tables for the event and spotted a cornhole set. His eyes lit up with excitement and we grabbed the bean bags to start playing. He likes to talk trash, so he immediately rambled on about how he was going to beat me. Three games later, he *still* hadn't won, and I had a smirk plastered on my face. There was no need to say anything.

The time came for the race to begin, and we lined up. I instructed him to stay with me since I was nervous about letting him take off on his own even though it was a simple route. The horn blew, and we started running. A lady in front of us dropped her earbuds on the ground just as we all took off, and she frantically tried to pick them up without getting run over by the stampede. Alex saw what happened and immediately ducked down to pick up her earbuds and handed them to her. Just as he did this, a large man who resembled a freight train with his size and speed didn't see him and almost collided with my little guy.

My heart froze as I gasped and watched the Freight Train barely miss Alex as he jumped over him and continued to run, both shocked and annoyed. I praised him for helping the lady but reminded him that he's smaller than the adults and needed to be *super* careful in situations like that so he wouldn't get run over. That would have been a bad collision for him. A half mile in, he started to get bored staying with me, because he wanted to run faster. Mom was too slow. I looked around at the other runners and assessed the situation.

"Okay, you can go off on your own when we hit 1 mile, but there are some rules. You HAVE to stay with the group, follow where all the people are running, and when you get to the finish line, stop immediately and wait for me there, I'll be right behind you."

He nodded, then spent the next half mile asking me every thirty seconds if we were at one mile yet. When we "finally" hit the one-mile marker, I nodded for him to go and reminded him of the rules.

"I will!" he said excitedly and broke away.

This was a milestone as a mom, letting him run the rest of the race without me. It was a delicate balance between letting him develop independence while being in a safe environment. I could see him ahead the rest of the way, but I wanted him to do his best. He's a natural-born endurance athlete like David, so I didn't want to hold him back.

What if I can't see him ahead of me?

That's why you dressed him in a bright shirt so you he's easy to find, he'll be fine.

As the race went on, I felt like I had to pee. In longer races like Half-Marathons and Marathons, there are pit stops along the route...but you will not likely see one in a 5k race since it is so short. This was not my first rodeo with feeling like I needed to use the bathroom during a race, so my inner voice chimed in to coach me along when I started to worry about it.

You're okay, this won't take long, and you can push through to the finish line.

This had happened before when I thought I had to pee during a race, but typically I had sweat out whatever fluids I was holding in and be okay until I finished. At one point I felt like a tiny bit may have leaked out, but I ignored it and focused on someone I saw running just ahead of me.

Hey, she looks like she is in my age group. Maybe I can pass her before we get to the finish line!

This is where my competitive nature comes in. At most races, I focus on my time, but I also want to do well if given a chance in my age group. This was like dangling a carrot in front of a horse. She was right in front of me, and I felt like I could do it. She was my carrot, and I *love* carrots. I continued to push as hard as I could without completely wearing myself out before the finish line. I still had to pee, but the feeling wasn't as strong. So, I kept going. The last part of the race was downhill, and I was thrilled. I'm one of those runners who makes goofy comments along the route, so if you're within earshot of me you'll probably hear some sort of comment that is equivalent to a dad joke come out of my mouth. My dad would be proud and say he taught me well.

"It's all downhill from here!!" I cried out loud as I felt the decline under my feet, slowly increasing my speed. We were nearing the finish line, and I was closing in on the woman in front of me. With 100 meters to go, the adrenaline came rushing in. I gave it everything I had and sprinted hard past her through the finish line.

YES!!!

Alex was there waiting for me with a medal around his neck. We walked over to the water station to grab bottles of water and to check our results to see if we needed to stick around for the awards. It turns out that the lady I passed *was* in my age group and passing her put me in third place. Mission accomplished! And surprisingly, I didn't need to pee anymore.

Huh, I guess I sweat it all out like before, or I was just overthinking like I tend to do.

We spent about 20 minutes walking around, talking to other runners, and introducing ourselves to the members of the Columbia Running Club that we had joined the previous month. After I blabbed on with some other people for a while, Alex asked if we could go home. He was getting hungry.

"Yep, let's go," I said to him, and we headed out.

I sat down in the car, put my phone in the seat, went to put my seatbelt on, and looked down in horror. My entire saddle area was completely drenched from the crotch down to the middle of both thighs.

Uhhhh, what is THIS??? Is that sweat?? PLEASE be sweat!!

Then, the realization hit me like a ton of bricks; or maybe like the Freight Train would have hit Alex.

OH MY GOSH, my entire bladder emptied during the race, and I didn't even know it!!!!

I sat there in complete shock and disbelief.

Is this real life? Am I dreaming??

Then, another realization sank in...

We just spent twenty minutes walking around talking to everyone after I peed all over myself!!! Wow, what a great first impression!

"Mommy, what are you doing?? Let's GO! I'm hungry!" Alex whined from the back seat.

"Dude, give me a second here!" I cried.

At first, embarrassment and mortification settled in, but then I started laughing hysterically. I could not *wait* to tell David.

Well, at least my running capris are all black and quick-drying material. I sure hope nobody noticed.

Who cares if they DID notice? This makes a funny story!!

This is quite comical.

I spent the rest of the drive home randomly laughing and asking myself, "Seriously?"

The second we walked in the door; I ran up to David. "You will *not* believe what just happened!!"

I told him how I peed myself and his jaw dropped in shock, then he started laughing hysterically as he looked down at my pants.

"This is what you married, a pee pot!! Aren't you lucky?!" I cried to him, laughing with tears streaming down my face. Then, another thought popped into my head.

Oh no, does this mean I have to wear pee pads every time I run a race??

So, off to Doctor Google I went to do some research about why I peed myself while running. A simple search pulled up information on SUI (Stress Urinary Incontinence). From what I was reading, it is quite common among middle-aged moms.

Fabulous.

I've made fun of my friends over the years who leaked a little bit when they laughed too hard, sneezed, or sometimes just breathed...but it wasn't a problem I had experienced yet. The Universe stepped in and decided to punish me for teasing them for so long.

Touche, Karma.

After reading how common it is, I overreacted and ordered a large batch of extra-absorbent pee pads from Amazon. This was my fate, to wear these mini diapers from now on when I ran in races.

It is what it is.

Is this the only answer to your problem? Let's investigate it a little more before you get

overdramatic and waste money on a ten-year supply of pee pads.

That's true. Let's go down some rabbit holes and see what we can find.

Stress Urinary Incontinence (or any urinary incontinence) is like many health issues...affected by inflammation. It's also extremely common for middle-aged women who have given birth.

Those dang kids.

Also, people with IBS have issues with SUI because of the amount of inflammation during a flare-up in the mid-section of the body. Hey, guess where the bladder is located? That's when the lightbulbs started going off with all the information I had learned over the years of struggling with my own health issues.

Wait a second; inflammation. Intermittent fasting reduces inflammation, especially in the midsection since it uses visceral fat for energy. Visceral fat is what surrounds the organs. What if I ran fasted to see if the same thing happened again? Diet, adequate sleep, and stress management can also help reduce inflammation. Oh gosh, there are SO many factors here, let's start playing around with this and do some experiments. I'd rather not have to wear a giant pee pad for every race because of this delightful new discovery.

Another few searches exposed menopause and its role in urinary incontinence. Perimenopause starts around the average age of 40-44 and lasts until your period officially goes away forever. Do you know how long this lasts on average? TEN YEARS!!!

But I thought menopause was just something that happened all at once when your period stopped!

What is this nonsense?? Why don't we talk about menopause? Why does it seem so shameful?

When girls start their periods, it's like this beautiful introduction to womanhood where they blossom into a flower and is a magical moment that is celebrated. With menopause, it's like women morph into crusty old witches who are shamed to hide in the corner with cobwebs and 37 cats until we wither away to nothing while casting curses on men for not having to deal with this mess. Shouldn't we be celebrating the fact that we don't have to go through our monthly Aunt Flo coming to visit? She is *exhausting!*

I remembered the first time I jumped on a trampoline after having kids. Once I got past the first few exhilarating jumps, it felt like my bladder was about to fall out of my bottom. That was the first time my inner child was very unhappy with the aging process.

After months of trial and error, the solution to my leaky bladder was reducing inflammation in my midsection. Daily intermittent fasting (13-17 hours) and limiting inflammatory foods (mainly gluten and refined sugar) helped me tremendously. I realized what triggered my issue with this lovely new discovery. Since there are multiple factors dealing with women's bodies as we go through this change in our lives, it took some finagling. When I run in the morning and fasted, I don't need a pee pad at all, and it's pretty much guaranteed that I won't have any leakage. If it's a longer or later race when I need to eat breakfast, there is a higher possibility of wearing one just as a backup, but it also depends on how many inflammatory foods I had eaten previously. Stress also causes inflammation, so there might be times when there's literally nothing I can do about it if I'm pushing way too hard. I'm not particularly excited to go through that again if I can avoid it, so I continued with trial and error as I learned more in the process.

Everything that happens in life is a learning experience, and it's great to be able to laugh at yourself. Life is boring without humor, and laughter is also really good for the abs. Your six-pack is hiding somewhere under there.

We had a lot to laugh about that day.

-24-

POST-RACE IBS FLARE-UP

We went to Pawleys Island for the Myrtle Beach Half-Marathon again for David's birthday weekend. I was thankful he's as nuts as I am with the running madness that he would be willing to spend his birthday weekend running a Half-Marathon. Who does that? *Crazy people.* However, the race nerves were fierce this time. I was so relaxed for the Daufuskie race, but it was different. We had a house full of people, including our kids, two new puppies, my parents, David's mom (Mimi), and her sister (SuSu). It was a full house.

Our bed was overly soft with no support, and the pillows were so thick that my neck felt like it had whiplash after the first night of sleep along with waking up sweating from not setting the AC to freezing. The weather was cold and rainy, not ideal for a weekend getaway at the beach. We couldn't leave our new puppies at the house by themselves since they would destroy anything they could get their little mouths on, and the kids were complaining about being inside too much because of the lousy weather. It wasn't an ideal trip, but we were still at the beach for the weekend.

Get it together; you and your first-world problems over here. You GET to be here. You GET to do this. You CHOSE to do this race and are ABLE to do it.

There it is, my reality check. Poor little me with my silly little problems. I am truly grateful to be here.

My eyes flew open the morning of the race, and I looked at the clock that read 1:15 am. My anxiety immediately spiraled to Level 10 on the Richter Scale.

WHY AM I AWAKE??? I have only been asleep for three hours! This bed is SO uncomfortable. The pillow is worse. My neck is killing me. The dogs are making too much noise. This is ridiculous, I HAVE to fall back asleep. I can't possibly run 13.1 miles on only 3 hours of sleep! Is it supposed to rain this morning like the weather said last night? I can handle running a 5k in the rain, but an extra ten miles seems like torture. I know I'm crazy, but that's on another level.

Take a deep breath and relax. The more worked up and anxious you are, the harder it will be to fall back asleep, and you need to rest.

Right. Relax, breathe, and focus on falling asleep. I can't possibly run that far on two nights in a row of terrible sleep, I'll end up getting sick. It's happened before. Wait, what time is it now? 2:48am. Are you kidding me?? My alarm is set for 4:00 so I have enough time to eat before the race starts at 6:35, I cannot run fasted for a Half-Marathon!!

Chill. Out. It's going to be okay. Even if you can squeeze in one more hour it will help.

Okay. I can fall back asleep. But what if it rains? Do I back out, or push through? Why does this race have to be so early?? Oh gosh, there will be so many people there, this is a big race and there are parking logistics to get to the start line. What time is it now? 3:40. I AM GOING TO CRY. I can't go back to sleep now; I have to eat before this race! Why can't I calm down?! Forget it, I need to check the weather and I'll go ahead and eat my breakfast.

It's going to be fine; you can take a nap later after you get back.

Okay Yoda, I get it. I know I'm spiraling and need to take a deep breath. This is going to be a great race! I love running through my hometown and may see someone I know! It's time to get up, put on my big girl panties, and get it done.

I pulled myself out of bed as quietly as possible, but the puppies jumped excitedly as they heard me get up in the darkness. Chewy jumped on me immediately, while Rocket launched his nose straight into my butt before I had a chance to put on pants to protect myself from being violated. Thank goodness for underwear. I jumped and concealed the squeal that came out of my throat, then swatted him away and fussed quietly.

I can't believe we thought bringing the dogs with us this weekend was a good idea, but they're puppies and not ready to stay with anyone else yet. Plus, they're so sweet and cute.

After navigating my way through the darkness, I brought the dogs with me into the living room. I grabbed my protein shake, oatmeal bar, a bottle of water, and headed to the couch. As expected, the dogs were pushing their way over who was able to smother me while I sat down and ate my breakfast. If you've never gotten a puppy, it's like having a toddler, and for some reason, we got *two* of them.

I waited until almost 5:00 to head back into our bedroom to get dressed. By now, it was about time for

David to start his process of waking up to eat breakfast and drink some coffee before we commenced our running torture for 13.1 miles in the rain.

"Is it raining?" he asked as he woke up.

"Yep."

"Oh no. You okay?"

"No. I only got 3 hours of sleep and I'm a good bit aggravated over it, but it'll be okay. I'll take a nap when we get back. I just hope I don't get sick from sleeping so terribly for two nights and then putting my body through the amount of stress this takes."

"It'll be fine, we'll be back before you know it."

We got ready, moving around as quietly as possible. He took the dogs out to do their business, we gathered our things and hopped in the car at 5:45 am in the pitch-black rain.

"What a beautiful morning for a run!" I said sarcastically, looking at the weather predictions.

It looked like the rain was going to lighten up shortly after the race started, so I crossed my fingers and toes just in case. Same as the previous year, we parked at Broadway at the Beach and headed to the start line by the Pelicans Baseball Stadium. This time, the port-o-potties were set up in a different location, right in front of a huge section of mud. We waited in line and navigated our way around the puddles like a game of hopscotch to relieve our bladders before starting.

"Are you going for your goal today?" I asked.

"Nah, I was going to run with you again if that's okay with you."

"Duh! Of course, it's okay!" I said with a smile and sense of relief. Running with him was more enjoyable.

The race began before we got to the start line, but we weren't concerned since we had our bibs with the chips to record our times. The rain stayed light and consistent, so my shoes were immediately wet. Fortunately, it stopped raining right at the 2-mile marker and we had cloudy skies the rest of the route. We chugged along, chatting occasionally along the way.

"So, are we going for under 2 hours today?"

"No, we are not!" I cried.

"Come on, you can do it!"

"Take a hike with that nonsense, unless you find a bike for me to ride!"

The run continued along fairly uneventfully during the first part, making our way down Hwy 17 Business, through Market Common, then onto Ocean Boulevard. This time, I was prepared with food and remembered to eat something at mile 6 instead of mile 10, and it made a significant difference in my energy levels. I made it to mile 10 before needing to make a pit stop, which was also a big improvement from the previous year.

Progress over perfection.
Baby steps for big babies.
Both statements are accurate.

The new route took a turn at mile 11 and took us to run along the boardwalk by the beach, which I hadn't experienced firsthand since it was built. The change in the surface went from running on asphalt to running on cement, and we started to feel the difference almost immediately after running for 11 miles. Cement is significantly harder than asphalt and provides less cushioning. This means it creates a harsher impact on the joints, especially the knees, hips, and ankles. Asphalt offers a little more give and can be gentler on your body over time, reducing the risk of joint pain and injury from repetitive pounding. Although the scenery was beautiful, we felt the impact for a little under a mile before the course turned again and put us back on asphalt. Almost to mile 12, David started to feel a sharp tightening in his left hamstring along with knee pain, and we had to slow down.

"You okay?" I asked.

"Yeah, I just need to walk for a minute. You go ahead, I don't want to hold you back."

"Boy, STOP! I am *not* leaving you after you have shuffled along with me for two races!"

"I know you want to improve your time."

"That's not important. I'm staying with you, end of story. Stop your silliness."

When we hit the last half mile, his motivation took over and he held a steady run to complete the race together. Although he was in pain, he was determined. We walked for one minute, then started running again. The pain crept in again more quickly, and we repeated this process a few more times before making the final turn. We ran through the finish line together, and I saw the time on my watch.

"We beat our last time by 3 minutes!" I cheered.

"But you could've gotten a better time if you hadn't stayed with my old, gimpy self!"

"STOPPIT!"

We grabbed bottles of water, mixed in some Liquid IV, and headed out. When we returned to the house, our families were waiting.

"How'd it go?" Mimi asked.

"We enjoyed it, but I am in desperate need of food and sleep," I replied.

"I don't know how y'all can run that far!" SuSu said, packing up her things to head home early.

After indulging in my muffin and coffee, I took a quick shower, headed to SuSu's empty bedroom, stripped down to a t-shirt, and immersed myself in the comfy bed for a nap. Shortly after I woke up, I recognized the pain I felt in my upper abdomen, and I knew exactly what was happening...an IBS flare-up.

The first time I had one was in my twenties, and I'd experienced them on and off for many years until a final diagnosis after three tests confirmed it was Irritable Bowel Syndrome. I was very familiar with the pain, and I knew it well. The discomfort ranged from a dull ache to intense, stabbing sensations in my upper abdomen. My doctor originally thought it was my gallbladder from the location of the pain, but an ultrasound revealed it was fine. Sometimes the pain came in waves, but other times it was constant and very difficult to find relief. All of my flare-ups over the years had been stress-induced, so the combination of two bad nights of sleep and my other anxiety and stress going on all at once with running the Half-Marathon was the icing on top of the cake. It was the perfect storm. And when you have OCD with anxiety that turns into panic attacks, the stress skyrockets, leading to a flare-up.

You know what you need to do. Take it easy, eat very light, healthy foods, and rest. The best thing you can do right now is to calm your mind so your body will follow suit.

I listened to the Yoda voice and spent a few days focusing on yoga, meditation, reading, relaxing, and light workouts. A Low FODMAP diet is helpful for me during a flare-up, so I was careful with what I ate to alleviate the inflammation as well. Within a week, the flare-up was completely gone and I felt back to normal, resuming everyday activities and training.

Every struggle comes with a lesson, and you can choose whether to learn from it and move forward or screw up again. Your choice.

Our furry toddlers, Chewy (left) and Rocket (right).

-25-

GOING OUT WITH A BANG

I woke up in the darkness and forgot where I was for a few seconds. That feeling is almost always alarming, not knowing where you are at first until the realization sets in. We were staying at a hotel in David's hometown for his favorite race of the year, the Run United event in Aiken. The room would have been quiet enough to hear a pin drop if I hadn't brought my sound machine, which leads me to a different subject.

Traveling is another fun part of aging. And when I say *fun*, I'm referring to the kind of fun you have when dealing with a toddler having a tantrum in the grocery store. Now that I'm in my forties, I love *my* bed in *my* bedroom in *my* house. The irony is that I also love traveling, but there are conditions with what needs to be packed. For example, my sound machine. When I was younger, I could sleep through a hurricane. I slept through Hurricane Hugo, to be specific. I slept through many more hurricanes living on the coast, along with countless other storms that could sink a toy boat in a bathtub. Part of this mid-life shift is needing that dang sound machine every time I sleep somewhere else. So, it goes with me every time I leave. We did this race the previous year for the first time, and completely fell in love with it. It's a big event in a small town, and you can see and feel the involvement of the community. The racecourses offer different distances (Half-Marathon, 10k, 5k, and even a Kids Fun Run), and are designed to showcase the beauty and charm of Aiken. Runners and walkers start and finish in the historic downtown area, winding their way through scenic neighborhoods, parks, and along shaded, tree-lined streets.

I looked at the clock, and it read 4:28 am. David was doing the Half-Marathon, which started at 7:30 along with the 10k, and the 5k started at 7:45 for me. I lay there, thinking about how this was the last race I would be running until I got an official diagnosis for my hip. I didn't want to make it any worse by running too much, and I knew it was time for a break. It didn't feel like I got *enough* sleep, but it was at least a solid 6ish hours. My body felt ready.

Well, this is your last race until you take a break from whatever is tweaking your hip. Make it a good one. Let's go out with a bang; without banging yourself up.

Since we ate dinner a little later than usual the night before and the race was earlier in the morning, I decided to fast. I got up and drank one bottle of water, followed by another bottle of water mixed with an LMNT electrolyte packet.

At the previous year's race, we stayed at a hotel within walking distance of the event. We didn't reserve early enough this year, so we had to drive a whopping ten minutes with minimal traffic. Although it was a short drive, it wasn't as phenomenal as being able to walk a few blocks to the start line. Once I had a taste of that luxury, it was hard to go back. I told David we were spoiled from the last year's hotel location.

We arrived in downtown Aiken in enough time to use the port-o-potty and socialize with a couple of coaches from Alex's Run Hard school team, both of them doing the Half-Marathon with David. It was a gorgeous morning, sunny with a slightly cool breeze and a temperature of 62 degrees. We couldn't have asked for better running weather. I attached my little Bluetooth speaker to my shirt, testing it out to make sure it was at the right volume.

"Why don't you just run with headphones if you want to listen to music?" David laughed at me.

"Because I want to be able to hear what's going on around me. The energy from everyone else fuels me, and I can't hear them if I stuff earbuds in my ears. This way, I get the best of both worlds!"

"You're silly."

"You do you, Boo."

The runners doing the Half-Marathon and 10k lined up for their race, and the energy built as everyone gathered around the start line. The liveliness surpassed most other races we had attended, which is why we see it as a standout event, return every year, and recruit others to join us as well.

The Run United event is a major fundraiser for the United Way of Aiken County. Proceeds from the race directly benefit local programs and initiatives focused on improving the lives of residents. By promoting health and wellness, the race encourages people of all ages and fitness levels to get involved, which makes it a truly inclusive community event. For a small town, the involvement is quite impressive. Even if people weren't participating in the races, they were volunteering at water stations or sprinkled along the routes with signs and cheering as runners passed by.

I felt great running along the course, watching my time and pacing myself as the mileage slowly piled up and I jammed along to my music. Since there were three distances, there were signs for which direction to take depending on your course. I thought about Alex, who complained he wasn't doing this one with us. Part of me felt guilty, but the other part knew that he could go the wrong direction and get lost downtown or end up accidentally running the Half-Marathon and be a puddle of goo at the end.

I feel guilty but would rather him wait until he's a little older, or someone else could run with him.

Don't feel guilty. You and David are doing this for yourselves, and he gets plenty of opportunities to run many races with both of you. Plus, he's doing his school 5k in two weeks.

During the last mile, I felt my body pushing against me, starting to wear out. I knew all too well that this was the time when mind over matter came into play, and it still fascinates me how powerful the mind can take over, especially in a physical situation. Even when my muscles started to feel tired and my legs began to ache, my mind could keep me moving forward. It's the mental strength that makes the biggest difference, helping me overcome physical fatigue. The brain can miraculously block out the discomfort, focusing on goals. I have noticed that when I believe I can push through, my body follows, proving that my mind is just as important as my physical endurance. I wanted to reach a PR (Personal Record), and it felt like it was the perfect day for it with the right combination of both physical strength and mental determination.

Just. Keep. Going.

I stopped looking at my watch after I hit the 2-mile mark and focused on the road in front of me as I continued moving one foot in front of the other. Going down the last straight shot of the course, I saw the finish line that was packed with spectators cheering along the route for the last quarter mile.

This is it. GO!!!

My pupils dilated, a smile spread across my face, and I broke into a sprint the last hundred meters. Although I've broken into a sprint multiple times when crossing the finish line, this time it felt different. I was stronger. Faster. Determined. I was so focused on doing my best and finishing strong that my body followed in line, pumping hard as I flew past other runners in front of me. The spectators cheered louder as I picked up speed, which fueled my adrenaline even more. I powered through the finish line, with an equal combination of exhilaration and exhaustion. It was the hardest I had pushed through a finish line, and I felt it in my body. It took me a couple of minutes to recover, walking around slowly and sipping on a bottle of water as I checked out the vendors and cheered for the other runners coming through to complete their distance.

I enjoyed watching others finish and could tell not only by the color of their race bib what course they were completing but also by how exhausted they were. David's goal for the day was to get his Half-Marathon time under 2 hours, so I eagerly anticipated his arrival because I knew he would be close to achieving it. Mimi, Kaitlyn,

Alex, and David's brother, Trey, came downtown to meet up and watch him finish. I kept checking his GPS along with the time and knew he would be cutting it extremely close. We saw him in the distance, and I gathered them up to be ready as he ran through the finish line.

"There he is!" I cried as I saw him approaching.

They piled along the side and cheered for him as he came running through the finish line.

"Don't crowd him when he gets over here, give him a minute," I instructed the kids.

He walked over toward us, taking time to catch his breath and come down from the exhaustion of pushing himself for 13.1 miles. Some runners are excited and energetic when they finish a race, while others are quiet and reflective. He is the latter. He took a minute to walk around slowly and stretch, and Alex handed him a bottle of water that I had mixed with a packet of Liquid IV.

"What was your time?" I asked.

"It was 2:00:44," he said and shrugged.

"Oh no! You barely missed it!"

"That's okay, I'll shoot for it next time. How did you do?"

"My fastest 5k time *ever* at 29:19!"

"That's great!"

"The timing was perfect with taking a break."

"You'll get back to it before you know it, and we'll get you to a sub 2-hour Half-Marathon," he smiled.

"Dream big, baby!"

Two weeks later when I woke up in the morning, I felt a mix of emotions flowing through me. It was the Spring Run Hard 5k for Alex and all the other kids in the Midlands area.

"I'm sorry bud, I won't be able to run the 5k this time," I said, sadly.

"Why not?" he asked, disappointed.

"Because I'm hurt and need to let my body rest. If I push too hard, I could make it worse and not be able to run for a very long time. Don't worry though, I'll be at the finish line waiting for you and Daddy to come in!"

"Okay!"

Since Alex started the program at his elementary school, I had been assisting the school's head coach, Dave, with over 100 kids who participated in the program. Although I was excited for him to do his race, I was disappointed that I wouldn't be running with him and all the other kids. I contemplated doing just one more race before taking a break but decided against it.

You need to take some time off and let your body heal. You got your best time, and David is running with Alex. Wait at the finish line for them.

Ugh. Why didn't I listen to my body when it was telling me what I should be doing MONTHS ago??

You cannot change the past. Focus on what you learned and move forward.

Fine. Dangit.

The four of us piled in the car and headed to Columbiana Mall on Harbison in Irmo for the race. The Run Hard program had grown exponentially, so much that Lexington and Richland had to have their own separate race because adding the surrounding counties became too massive. It had also spread to a couple of other states, and I hope it continues to grow. I have seen so much of the positivity it gives kids, and I recommend it to every parent I talk to about trying one season to see how their child likes it. Although it was only two counties worth of schools, there were still *hundreds* of runners. I cannot sing praises enough about this program, which is why Alex loves doing it every season, and I tag along as an assistant coach. We found a parking spot about half a mile away from the start line and watched as hundreds of cars pulled into the parking lot.

"Oh my gosh! Look at all these people!" I cried.

They lined up to start, and the number of runners doubled with each child having a Buddy Runner (an adult or teenager to run with them). The music pumped loudly, and Coach Jesse got them all riled up, ready to run their little hearts out. The horn blew, and I watched the massive amount of runners take off. I squeezed myself into a spot at the finish, sat down on the pavement, and eagerly anticipated the runners to come in. I took videos and pictures of the kids finishing their race, pushing themselves to the max. I felt excitement radiate through my heart as I saw David and Alex come through the finish line with his fastest time ever of 26:41.

I want to run with them, so we can all cross the finish line together someday...but I'll need to get better. I have to train much harder than both of them to have half a chance to keep up. I wonder if I can.

You don't know if you don't try.

The gorgeous tree-lined streets in downtown Aiken provide scenery and shade along the route. We look forward to this race every year.

-26-

THE FOUNTAIN OF YOUTH IS DRY

It was Spring of 1987, and I sat in a warm bathtub with my strawberry-blonde hair stuck to my head as I played with toys and bubbles. I had a habit of staying in the tub until it got too cold, then scrambled to get out to dry off and warm up again. Sometimes, I would sneak more hot water into the tub to prolong having to get out. When I stood up to get out of the bath, my mom noticed something amiss on my body.

"What is it?" I asked her as she gently pressed two bumps on my upper groin area.

"I don't know, we'll go to the doctor and ask."

For Christmas, Santa brought me a Heart-To-Heart Bear. It was a popular stuffed animal in the eighties, and she was my new companion. She kept me company and slept in the bed with me every night, especially since she was wearing pink and white striped pajamas with a little hat. When you pressed on her chest, you would feel the thump of her heartbeat from a small heart-shaped contraption inside. I was obsessed with stuffed animals with a growing collection, and one of them went with me to many places regularly. So, it wasn't a surprise that I wanted to take her with me to my appointment.

"She has a heartbeat!" I told the doctor excitedly when he asked about her.

"She does?!" he exclaimed, not believing me. He had never seen the bear before and didn't know they existed, so he was in for a surprise.

"Yes! Listen to it!" I exclaimed and held her out for him to listen with his stethoscope.

He smiled and decided to play along, holding the stethoscope to her chest and pressing down. I felt her heart start to beat in my hands as he listened. His face dropped, and his eyes widened. He looked up at me, then at my mom in complete shock.

"Wha- What *is* this thing?" he asked.

"It's a Heart-To-Heart Bear!" I exclaimed.

We pulled the heart out of her chest to show him.

"I was *not* expecting that!" he replied.

We all laughed and went on with our appointment for him to examine what was on my groin. When he explained to my mom what was going on, I was lost. I didn't know what he said I had, and I didn't know what surgery was. I sat in silence and waited until we got in the car for her to explain what was happening.

"You'll need to have surgery, and very soon," she said. She looked worried, which was unusual for her.

I had a double inguinal hernia. An inguinal hernia, often referred to as a groin hernia, happens when a portion of the abdominal contents pushes through the inguinal canal and protrudes into a weak spot in the abdominal wall near the groin. This can occur if an opening in the muscle wall fails to close properly before birth, leaving a vulnerable area that can bulge when subjected to pressure.

Although they're not always dangerous, they can grow and lead to life-threatening complications. The doctor suspected mine had been there since birth and had grown over the years, which was why there was an urgency to have surgery.

"Can I still have my birthday party this summer?" I asked her.

Birthdays were big in our family, and I couldn't miss my 7th birthday. She smiled and said, "Of course."

We went in for an appointment to meet with the surgeon to review all the details we needed to know before the big day.

"When you go in the operating room, you'll see a green balloon. When I tell you to blow up the balloon, you're going to blow as hard as you can to try and pop it!" the surgeon said with a smile. "And if you pop the green balloon, you can have all the money in my wallet!"

My eyes grew big, and I smiled at my mom.

As soon as we left, I said excitedly to her, "I bet he has a lot of money in his wallet, he's a *doctor*!"

"I bet so!" she laughed.

The day of surgery came, and I was absolutely terrified. My mom's calm demeanor helped ease my nervousness until they peeled me away from her. I didn't cry though, because I was tough; that's what my dad and brothers had told me. The nurses rolled me into the operating room, and I looked around in wonder at all the gadgets. The room was cold and intimidating, filled with strange machines with lots of different noises. Everyone was wearing scrubs, masks, and caps on their heads. When my bed was situated for surgery, the doctor leaned over and looked at me. I could see his eyes crinkled up from smiling.

"Okay, are you ready?" he asked.

I stared back at him silently and nodded my head. I wasn't known for being silent very often, but this was one of those rare times when I didn't say a single word.

"Remember to pop the green balloon, it's right there!" he pointed behind him.

There it was; the green balloon in all its glory...the color of money in the surgeon's wallet. I wanted it.

"Okay!" I said with a smile. I was determined to pop that balloon. I took the deepest breath I had ever taken and blew as hard as I could into the mask. The balloon got very big, but it didn't pop.

Dang! Try again, but this time pop it!

As I sucked in air from the mask, my mind set on popping that balloon on the second attempt, I inhaled the anesthesia. Not even halfway into blowing up the balloon on the second try, I passed out.

When I woke up, I felt groggy and was unaware of where I was. I looked around the large room with other patients who were also on stretchers. The pain I felt was intense, unlike anything I had experienced.

"Where's Mommy? It *hurts!*" I whined over and over again. Although the nurse told me I would see her soon, the pain was excruciating and all I wanted was the comfort of having my mom there. After the first ten times I asked, the nurse became a little worn out.

At the time, my parents owned a small medical transport business with ambulances that transferred patients to and from different locations that were non-emergencies. My dad showed up at the hospital driving an ambulance, ready to take his little girl home on a stretcher. When they brought me out of the recovery room, they transferred me to a little red wagon as a special treat. Although I always enjoyed riding in red wagons, I was uncomfortable and in a lot of pain. They carefully transferred me back to a stretcher from the wagon and put me in the back of the ambulance. The nurses standing by were confused about why this little girl was riding home in an ambulance instead of loading her into a car.

I laid on the couch for almost a week, missing school. Although I enjoyed watching cartoons, I loathed being stuck on the couch and unable to play. Several of my neighborhood friends came by to visit, along with other family members. Both of my brothers were abnormally doting and volunteered to get me whatever I needed during that time. It was short-lived and I thought they were possessed by some sort of aliens, but also appreciated their weird kindness. All returned to normal when I was able to run around again in a couple of weeks, and they went back to acting like regular old stinky big brothers.

In December 2023, my groin had been abnormally tight for about a month and was progressively getting worse. Although the pain was mild, it was enough to notice that something was wrong and started radiating through to my lower back. That is one of the most fascinating things I have learned about overall health, is being in touch with my body and knowing when something is off. When you feel lousy *all* the time, it's hard to notice when something isn't right. However, when you feel good and healthy, it's easier to catch an injury or illness before it spirals out of control into something more serious.

What in the world is going on with my right groin? I hope I don't have a hernia again.

The thought of having surgery in my forties wasn't appealing at all, especially since it was more common at my age.

Wow, that makes me feel even older, at my age.

You won't likely have a hernia, but it would be a good idea to get it checked out.

Sometimes, it's hard not to catastrophize, especially when I knew that injuries affect an average of 70% of runners per year. And let's face it: I went from zero running to a crazy, wanna-be endurance athlete. It was a big shift for a body only used to minor workouts, like walking, easy weight training, and yoga.

"I think it's a strained iliopsoas. I can refer you to an orthopedist or start you on physical therapy to see if that helps, whatever you prefer," my doctor said when I went in for an appointment.

"I'd like to start with physical therapy."

The first physical therapist I saw was like my chiropractor; not a fan of running. I'd already read many books written by ultrarunners (extra-crazy centaurs who run hundreds of miles for races) who put their bodies through more than my little brain could fathom. If running is really that bad for you, how are millions of people able to do it their entire lives?

I thought a proper balance of cross-training and strength training can keep you running healthily for many years. Are they just simply not fans of it?

They could have a negative personal experience from it that they never grew from. Figure out what works best for YOUR body, and

you do you, Boo. Don't worry about what anyone else thinks about it.

After the mandatory 4 weeks of physical therapy, my orthopedic doctor ordered an MRI to determine exactly what was going on with my right hip. The only time it aggravated me from running was if I ran a lot of hills, which I didn't do often. When the MRI came back, it diagnosed several issues:

-Chondromalacia (cartilage wear and tear)

-Cam-type osteophyte (bone spur that may cause friction and damage to the hip joint)

-Fraying of the Labrum (due to degeneration from Osteoarthritis)

-Early signs of tendinosis in muscles that support the hip (degeneration of tendons)

Whew, that's multiple things all going on at once. This is not the kind of multi-tasking I like. Now what do I do to fix it?

Growing up, I was a "why" kid. When an adult explained a smidge of information, I would pipe in and ask, "Why?" to get a deeper understanding of what they were saying. As an adult, this inquisitiveness consistently leads me down many rabbit holes looking for more information to understand different subjects and issues. If something is wrong, I not only want to understand why it's wrong or what caused it, but also how to fix and prevent it from happening in the future. A mistake is something you make when you don't know better, but a bad choice is something you make when you *do* know better; yet choose to ignore the consequences. I used to do the latter but have grown into the former. Making the same mistakes over and over again is like smacking yourself repeatedly in the head with a frying pan, and then complaining about having a headache. Why take meds for a headache when you could just stop smacking yourself in the head with the frying pan? I feel like prevention is a subject that is not discussed enough. I used to want a quick-fix remedy rather than getting to the root cause of the problem and preventing it but developed a different outlook.

Let's go down some rabbit holes to find the root cause to properly heal and prevent issues as much as I can in the future.

Chondromalacia is the softening and deterioration of the cartilage, which is a common feature of Osteoarthritis. A Cam-type Osteophyte causes friction in the hip joint, particularly during movement. Degenerative fraying of the labrum means it is starting to wear out and become damaged, from Osteoarthritis and possible impingement from the Cam-type Osteophyte. Tendinosis results in the breakdown of collagen fibers in the tendons, showing early signs of wear and damage at their attachment points. After speaking to my orthopedist, she confirmed the main culprit was Osteoarthritis.

Am I just supposed to stop running and sit in the living room on a recliner and wait to keel over? I don't think so.

Since it was caught relatively early, there was no need for surgery, and steroid shots would only be necessary if the pain became severe. I decided against the steroid shots since the pain was somewhat mild, and pain is also an indicator of something being wrong. So, how would I know it was improving if the pain and discomfort were covered up with a shot? I wasn't fully against it, but also wanted to explore other options first.

After reaching out to my local running group for recommendations, I found another physical therapist with a PhD who was a marathoner and specialized in both strength training and running rehabilitation. She was the perfect fit. When I went in for my first visit, I noticed a framed document on her wall with a familiar logo and gasped when I saw it.

"You've done an *Ironman*??"

"I have!" she smiled.

An Ironman Triathlon consists of a 2.4-mile swim, a 112-mile bike ride, and a 26.2-mile run...all together. This confirmed I was in the right hands.

As I expected, the intuition that had yelled at me months before to incorporate more strength training into my routine was correct. Using weights doesn't just strengthen your muscles, it also strengthens your bones, tendons, ligaments, and joints. The puzzle pieces were coming together with the root cause of my issues.

Six months before developing the pain and discomfort, I decided to switch my running shoes. I went from shoes that had cushion, support, and a 10mm drop to minimalist shoes, with zero-drop and almost no cushion and support. I loved my Altra zero-drop shoes, and they seemed to improve my running mechanics, but the problem was that I needed more cushioning for shock absorption while running on the road. The shoes I had been running in worked on the treadmill, but I needed more support for hard surfaces. As expected, I needed shoes with a lot more cushion for road running than what I had been using, and I couldn't get a new pair fast enough. I ordered a pair almost identical to the ones I had been using, but with maximum cushioning and it made a big difference. Lesson learned.

You don't know what you don't know, and you have learned from your mistakes. Take this information with you and make the right choices for the future.

Before the diagnosis, I had a gut feeling one day about what I "should" have been doing. While doing another lower body strength training workout, I knew deep down what I needed to focus on.

You have to prioritize strength training. You know how crucial it is.

I know, but I want to RUN! And it interferes with how many miles I can go in a day!

It's not all about running. Slow your roll, girl. You're not doing as much strength training as you need, and you know you feel better doing it. Plus, you love how strong you get from it!

I know...but...RUNNING!!!

If at any time my inner voice rolled its eyes at me, that was it. I spent the summer focusing on a lower body strength training plan my physical therapist put together for me, and I went in every few weeks to evaluate the progress. In the meantime, I had to take time off from running until my body was ready to ease back into it. That part was more challenging than I expected.

Taking eight weeks off from running felt like an emotional rollercoaster. At first, I tried to stay positive, telling myself it was just a small setback, and that rest would help me heal. But as the days stretched into weeks, the frustration began to build. Running had become my outlet—a way to relieve stress, clear my mind, and feel strong. Without it, I felt lost. Watching others run, whether on social media or in the neighborhood, was tough. I missed the feeling of lacing up my shoes, the sense of freedom when my feet hit the pavement, and the accomplishment of finishing a long run. Instead, I was stuck in a cycle of resting, icing, and physical therapy exercises, all while wondering if I'd ever get back to the level I was at before. There were days when I felt emotionally defeated, doubting if my hip would fully heal or if I'd ever enjoy running again.

The hardest part was the uncertainty. Each day off felt like progress slipping away, and I worried that my fitness would vanish completely. The emotional toll was as heavy as the physical, as running had become a huge part of my routine and my identity. It was my crazy medicine, and I needed it. It felt like a piece of me was missing, and the idea of rebuilding from scratch once I recovered was daunting.

Through it all, I realized how much running meant to me—not just as exercise, but as a source of strength, confidence, and joy. The eight weeks felt like forever, and while my body needed the rest, my mind struggled with the absence. But in the quiet moments, I learned patience and resilience, knowing that when I finally returned, I would appreciate every step even more. I couldn't wait to start training again and became so engulfed that I neglected chiropractic adjustments.

When I scheduled an appointment, I hadn't been in three months. That's a long time to go when your body is used to getting adjustments, but I had been putting it off. Between the diagnosis, physical therapy, and an erratic summer schedule with the kids, time slipped away from me. I explained the frayed labrum and aggravation of my iliopsoas muscle. After doing an evaluation, it was just as I had expected; my hips were significantly out of alignment. He did a few adjustments, then applied heat to my lower back.

The next day, my *left* hip felt off. As the day continued, it got worse. I took some ibuprofen before bed to see if that would help. When I woke up the following morning, I was miserably uncomfortable. Both my hip flexors felt extremely tight, and I could only take small steps while walking. After consulting Doctor Google, it said this was normal from an adjustment (especially since they were so out of whack from months of my body nursing an injury), so the muscles, tendons, and ligaments were adjusting to the new position, taking a few days for everything to feel mobile and fluid again.

This is why you should stay consistent with the adjustments. When your body was adjusted regularly to make sure your hips were in alignment, it was used to it. You went too long without them.

How long will it take me to listen to this new perspective ALL the time?

Think about how far you have progressed. Change doesn't happen overnight, it takes time.

Why are you so logical?

Because sometimes you need a lovable kick in the butt to keep you moving forward.

Although it took time, it shifted my perspective (yet again) on prioritizing my health. Even though I still had no wild aspirations of becoming an elite runner, I had learned so much about what it did for my mental, physical, and emotional health that I wasn't going down without a fight. Making excuses wasn't an option, and I was willing to improvise and shift to do what it required to keep moving forward. This was merely a speed bump, not an endpoint. I learned many valuable lessons from this injury that contributed to my growth and experience and took them with me on my journey.

From this, I learned:

-Prioritize strength training.

-The right kind of shoes are crucial.

-Progress *slowly* with mileage; this is for an improved quality of life.

- Incorporate more cycling, swimming, pickleball, HIIT (High Intensity Interval Training) so my body is used to moving in different directions.

-Stay consistent with chiropractic adjustments.

-Youth is wasted on the young.

-Proper rest and recovery are deal-breakers.

-Eating junk makes me feel like junk.

-Being able to run races brings me more joy than I realized it did.

-When I stopped running, my resting heart rate increased.

-Although I continued to run at turtle speed, I was still moving forward and that mattered so much more than my race times.

Wow, that was a lot.

Everything in life happens for a reason, and you've grown from these lessons. Remember to have patience, Baby Yoda.

-27-

A NEW PERSPECTIVE ON RACING

"Okay, it's time to head to the track!" I told Alex on a Saturday morning.

"Do I have to go?" he asked, staring at his iPad.

"Yes! The 5K is in *two* days!"

I see screens as both a blessing and a curse. Although the kids can do and learn some amazing new things from them, I can also see their brains rotting in front of my eyes with some of the games and videos they watch. This is why they are not allowed unlimited time on these gadgets or on school days. I am a mean mom who has no problem saying the dreaded word: NO.

"We're only going to be there for thirty minutes. Somehow you'll survive; I just know it!"

I'd spent the summer focused on strength training and easing back into running to avoid tweaking my hip. This whole aging thing is not for the faint of heart, although I'm very thankful to have the opportunity to do so. Easing back into running meant slow jogging, with no sprints or hard runs.

"I'm just going to walk while we're out here," he said when we got to the track.

"That's fine, do what you want to do. Either way, we're out here for thirty minutes."

We set our water bottles on a bench and started walking around to warm up. Since we train differently, going to the track makes it easy since we're at the same location, but we can both go at our own speed. I walked one lap around, then started jogging at a slow pace. He wasn't ready for a big training session, so he stayed with me. When I jogged, he jogged. When I walked, he walked. We rounded for a third lap and passed the start line for the 100-meter sprint. My body was warm, and a thought flickered in my mind, and I looked at him.

"Hey, you wanna race?"

His face lit up.

"YES!!!"

"Go!" I cried, and we took off at full speed.

We stayed toe-to-toe, sprinting together down the track. I saw him coming up closer to me as we approached the finish line, and I pushed harder to keep ahead of him, finishing first. He stared at me in shock, catching his breath.

"Wow, you got *faster*!" he said.

"Of course I did, we were sprinting!"

He had only seen me jog slowly and knew his 5k pace was faster than mine. He assumed my limited jogging abilities were only at a geriatric speed. Halfway around another lap, I felt a slight pull in my bum hip.

Today may not have been the best day to take off like that, so let's take it easy until after the race.

I figured that would happen and should have known better...but it also felt great to show my little man that his old mom could actually *run*.

"Can we do that again?" he asked.

"Maybe later, we'll see."

As we continued to jog, I felt another pull in my

hip and decided it would be best to hold off on that again for the day to avoid further injury.

"We'll sprint the next time we come up here, I promise."

"Okay," he nodded. He wanted a rematch.

Two days later, our family piled in the car and headed to downtown Columbia for the Labor Day 5k.

"I appreciate you running with your cousin, but he hasn't trained as much as you have. Please don't push him too hard," I said to Zack as we warmed up.

Last Spring, he ran with another boy in the same grade as Alex in the Run Hard 5k School Race. The other boy trained regularly by playing soccer and did quite well with running the 5k. The boy's mom encouraged Zack to help her son to place at the top of his age group, so he obliged. He ended up placing, but the poor little guy was pushed harder than expected and wasn't feeling so hot afterwards. Since Alex doesn't play soccer and hadn't been training much, I wanted to make sure I had an anti-pep talk with Zack, so he didn't do that in this race.

"So, you're saying you want him to run it in less than 21 minutes?" he smiled.

"Not today!" I cried and poked him in the side.

The four of us lined up together and waited. I registered Zack to run with Alex so David and I could focus on our times, and it also gave him a reason to train in the off-season from track. Grammy and Kaitlyn were there for support and waited close to the finish line. I knew that since this was my first 5k in over four months, I wouldn't be going for a personal best time. The training I did all summer was light and easy due to my hip injury, which did not include any hill work. This course was described as flat and fast, but it was *not* a course I would consider flat. The race went along as I expected, I just took it easy and coached myself along the way to stay steady. It was harder than I anticipated, mostly because of those dang rolling hills I wasn't prepared for. In the last mile of the race, I came upon a young girl running by herself. She was going back and forth between sprinting and walking, passing me as she ran and me passing her as she walked.

"You've got this!" I called out to her.

"Do you know how much farther we have left?"

"Just over half a mile. You're welcome to stay with me and sprint through the finish line at the end!"

"Okay!"

She ran with me as we got closer to the finish, and we chatted along the way.

"There it is! Do you see it? GO!" I cheered.

She took a deep breath and picked up her speed. As I watched her break away, I wondered if I would also be able to shift into a sprint closer to the finish line.

Don't try to keep up with her, you don't want to hurt yourself just getting back into it. She's only ten, you deal with stuff she doesn't have nightmares about yet.

About 50 yards from the finish line, I picked up some speed and pushed through. It certainly wasn't my personal best time, and it wasn't easy getting back into it since all my runs had been light, but it felt *terrific* to cross the finish line again. It reminded me of my first race since I wasn't focused on my time, even though I had a watch. The best part was no bladder leakage, and that's always a win in my book.

"How did you know that lady and her daughter you were talking to?" David asked on the way home.

"I didn't. I saw the girl getting worn out from sprinting and walking, so I encouraged her to stay with me. I talked to her and her mom after."

He laughed.

"What?! There has not been a race when I *didn't* speak to someone along the course!" I exclaimed.

"And there has not been a race when I *did* speak to someone along the course!"

"Shocker!" I teased.

As I stared out the window on the car ride home, I thought about how enjoyable it was to complete a race without worrying about pace or time...just being there for the experience.

I want more of this. I want to do more races where I'm just there to enjoy the environment. It's great to have goals, but it was more fulfilling just being there. Being ABLE to do it. I'm so grateful for that.

After we got home, I did what I always do after checking the race results; looked for more events. Earlier in the year, I came across some gravel bike races through Southeast Gravel's website. These are off-road bicycle races with different distances available. The Spring events conflicted with other plans we had going on during the year, so I kept an eye on the Kershaw Gold Rush race in Heath Springs in the Fall. As I looked over the site, I got nervous and wondered if I could do it. This was completely different than all the other events I had done so far.

I'm a little scared.
What are you scared of?

The unknown. I'm a suburban girl and have never done anything off-road like a gravel race, trail run, or even camping. I'm a glamper, not a camper.

You're looking at them, which means you're interested.

Of course, I am, there's something that draws me to them but I'm not sure what it is.

Choose the shortest distance and go with David, that way you'll be able to step outside your comfort zone yet still feel safe.

I'll talk to him and see what he thinks.

"The gravel bike race I told you about is coming up in less than three weeks. It's 13 miles, off-road, so we'll be on our bikes for approximately an hour and a half, give or take a few minutes. What do you think?"

"I'm up for it if you want to go, so you decide."

The next thing I knew, we were registered. This was a brand-new territory with it being in a rural setting and we needed to upload the GPS on a phone to tell us where to go. This was going to be an adventure.

That's a good thing, it gives your life experience and allows you to do something different and see if this is something you'd be interested in doing more of. It's time to get acquainted with your beloved mountain bike again.

That's right. I know my legs will be tired, and I must get my bottom used to riding again to avoid sore giblets after the race. Let's do this.

Those who run together stay crazy together.

-28-

HITTING THE TRAIL

 Six days before the gravel bike race, we loaded all four bikes on the truck and drove to Saluda Shoals Park in Irmo for a family ride. Although I felt confident in my and David's endurance capacity for the upcoming race, my creampuff bottom had not yet been fully conditioned to ride on a bike for over an hour. We love taking the kids with us on these leisurely rides, but my inner child still wants to take off at full speed and I am forced to reel it in. I wondered if self-control in this aspect would get me closer to the Mother of the Year award, but it's still not quite close enough.

 As we got our bikes unloaded and ready to go, I set my watch to keep track of time and mileage. I was more concerned about time rather than distance since conditioning my bottom was the top priority for the day. I knew I could handle pushing hard on the bike much better than running.

 "Y'all ready?" I asked.

 "Let's GO!" Alex cried.

 We exited the parking lot and rode toward the main paved path of the park. It's a long stretch that goes down about a mile and a half before running into the Saluda River, where you have to turn around. I was in the lead, with Alex, Kaitlyn, and David behind me. I went into paranoid Mommy Mode and insisted the kids be sandwiched in between us while riding. I kept peeking back to make sure they were close, with Alex on my heels (or tire, I should say) and the other two a little ways back. Kaitlyn enjoys the slow rides, while Alex and I are speed demons together when we get going. As we rode along, I thought about the race ahead and became more excited. The fear I had while first signing up had morphed into anticipation, and I couldn't wait.

This is going to be a new experience!

After riding about three miles, I noticed Kaitlyn and David had gotten farther behind us, so I stopped for them to catch up.

"You okay?" I asked her.

"Yeah. Can we not go up any more hills?"

"I can try, but I have no control over what the ground does along the path!"

This was a form of exercise our sweet dancer wasn't used to, and the "hills" she was referring to were small inclines. We continued riding at a slower speed, and I looked behind me more frequently to make sure I wasn't leaving them in my dust again. I turned off the main path onto a smaller, shaded one.

I need to attach a rearview mirror on this bike.

We rounded a curve and came up on a couple walking with their dogs, who had stopped. The man was ahead of the woman, standing in the middle of the path, and cautiously looking at something to the side. He looked my way and held his hand up for me to stop. My intuition screamed at me.

It's a copperhead snake.

A chill went down my spine as I immediately hit the brakes, with Alex right behind me.

"Is it a snake?" I called out.

"Yes, it's a copperhead."

I knew it.

"Oh, a copperhead!" Alex cried and rode past me, closer to the couple to see for himself. The child is fascinated with snakes, and my anxiety exploded like a Mentos was tossed into a 2-liter Coke bottle.

"Alex, *STOP!!*" I screamed at him.

"Why? I want to see it!"

"STOP RIGHT NOW!!!"

He slowed down to a turtle speed, inching up to get just a little closer. I'm convinced no day goes by when this kid is looking for a loophole in every situation presented to him.

I joined a local Facebook group that identifies snakes in the state of South Carolina so I could learn more about identifying them. We see large rat snakes who are well-fed in our neighborhood, and I snapped a picture of one while driving down the street one day. I believe my fear in many situations is based on my lack of knowledge about whatever I'm afraid of, which is why I want to learn more. If I see a rat snake that I know is not going to come after us, I'm more relaxed. It's not snakes I fear in general; specifically *venomous* ones. Those fears are amplified if one of my children goes anywhere near them.

David passed us and kept Alex behind him as they got within a safe, close distance to see it. My heart pounded as I watched Alex, and then I let out a sigh of relief when they confirmed it had slithered back away from the path. Kaitlyn stayed behind me, with no interest in getting anywhere near it. As we continued riding for

for another thirty minutes, I thought about this fear, and how it had prevented me from enjoying nature more often.

Your anxiety is derived from a lack of knowledge and experience with nature. You've always been a suburban girl, so it's time to step outside your comfort zone. Take the time to learn more and try new things.

I slept well the night before the race and woke up excited. As I made my way to the bathroom, I discovered it was the first day of my *least* favorite week of the month. It was a minor inconvenience, but I chuckled at the timing. I woke David up at 6:00, and he groaned it was too early to get up. Mimi had spent the night with us to stay with the kids while we drove an hour and a half to the race site for our little field trip.

As we rode down the interstate at almost 80 mph, his bike which was carefully strapped to the rear-mounted bike rack began to loosen. At first, the straps were secure, but the constant vibrations from the road and strong gusts of wind gradually worked them loose. Suddenly, one of the straps gave way, causing the bike to shift and pull on the other straps, loosening them as well. Suddenly, the bike detached from the rack, and David noticed quick movement in the rearview mirror when the wheels dropped, and saw his bike barely hanging on by a thread with the handle stuck between the wheel and frame of my bike.

"The bike! It's falling off!!" he cried, immediately hit the brakes and pulled off to the shoulder. There was a deep embankment along the shoulder, so the safety rails made it a very narrow place to pull over.

My stomach jumped into my throat as I nervously watched him hop out of the truck, run to the back, and adjust his bike to put it back on the rack. My heart raced as he worked at lightning speed, hoping he could fix it quickly and get back into the truck. Another truck flew by rather close, causing him to jump and I about fainted. He finished strapping the bike to the rack, then hopped back into the driver's seat.

"Talk about an adrenaline rush I wasn't expecting before the race!" I exclaimed.

"I'm so glad I saw it when I did! I don't know what happened, it was strapped on *tightly*. I'm so glad it didn't come all the way off and hit a car behind us!"

He kept a close eye out as we approached the exit off the interstate, then pulled into a gas station to reassess and strapped an extra bungee cord around both bikes, securing them even more.

We drove through the country, following the map coordinates for Brewer Plantation. It was 2,500 acres of land that had been in the family since the mid-1700s. This event was number 5 out of 6 for Southeast Gravel during the year and is one of their most popular races. The course was filled with a variety of paths, filled with dirt, grass, gravel, rocks, pavement, and some harsh inclines. We arrived only ten minutes before the race started, and I made a mental note that we should leave much earlier next time. My anxiety is not a fan of being rushed to the start line.

The Long Course consisted of 49 racers going 83 miles and took the start at 9:00 am. The Short Course had 123 racers going 45 miles starting at 9:05, and then 9 of us completed the Fun Course of 13 miles at 9:10. We stood far enough ahead of the long racers so I could take some video of the first groups as they took off, and I was mesmerized. Although I was used to viewing serious runners as centaurs, I rarely had an opportunity to see serious *cyclists* up close and personal.

"I don't see anyone else with mountain bikes like we have, they all have gravel bikes," David noticed as we watched them ride by.

"I'm not worried about that today, I think our bikes will be fine on this course, especially since this is our first one."

The start of the course was about a 1.5-mile-long path of sand. There were parts of hard-packed and loose sand, and we had to navigate carefully to avoid going through the soft parts and losing control of the bike. It was a new maneuvering obstacle, and I took my time since the thought of face-planting wasn't particularly desirable. Although the route was marked with signs, they strongly recommended we download the GPS route on our phones to prevent us from getting lost. Since we planned to stay together, David had the route on his phone and stayed just ahead of me. After the sand trail, we turned right onto a rural country road and continued for about a half mile before turning onto a wide, gravel path in the woods. At first, it wasn't too challenging, just a lovely ride through nature as I soaked in the beauty of the entire experience.

The casual ride shifted when we started going through steady inclines and declines, constantly shifting gears on our bikes. The inclines both increased and intensified, followed by a relieving decline where we could coast and enjoy the breeze. I was sure they weren't tough inclines for experienced cyclists, but I was far from being experienced.

This is SO much harder than I expected it to be!

Girl, you're only 4 miles into the ride, you've got a ways to go.

I know, but DANG! I was not expecting this at all! I thought riding was my strength!

Natural ability will only take you a short distance, it's the hard work that propels you to success and accomplishments.

I need to strengthen my lower body, bigtime!

Then do it!

I will!

We continued along the course with constant ebbs and flows of pushing uphill and coasting downhill. Every section of wincing in pain from pushing too hard was followed by a sigh of relief when the ground shifted in the opposite direction. It was a wild ride.

This is INCREDIBLE!!!

I powered along, losing sight of David a few times ahead of me before catching up to him again on the declines. His natural strength and endurance were really showing up in this race, and he was enjoying every second of it just as much as I was.

"This is such a struggle! And I LOVE it!!" I cried when I caught up to him.

"Isn't this great?!" he exclaimed.

Who have I become? Enjoying the struggle? Who is this person in my body now?

When I was younger, my mindset saw struggle as both exhausting and annoying. I greatly preferred ease over challenge, and the new shift was spectacular.

I knew a paved road was coming ahead and was ecstatic. Going fast on paved roads was ten times easier than on the off-road paths, and I wanted to get some speed going. I shifted gears and pedaled faster, feeling the breeze and a grin spread across my face like the Grinch on Christmas morning. The feeling of exhilaration was overwhelming as I pedaled my heart out on this rural road. I wasn't afraid of cars, critters, or crashing. I was truly enjoying every single ounce of the experience on the ride, even the periodic inclines on the road. Those 3 ½ miles went by quickly before turning onto a narrow trail in the woods. We stopped briefly to take a breather before tackling the last part of the course, and I drank some water. A lady coming up behind us on her bike had done this race before and told us the photographer took pictures of each person on the insane incline ahead.

"How ironic!" I laughed.

As I pedaled through the forest on a grass path, the sight of David and his bike ahead began to fade. With every twist and turn, we became farther apart. Suddenly, I found myself alone on the trail, unsure of which path he had taken at a fork in the route. My heart raced as I debated which direction to go, worried I might get further lost if I chose the wrong way.

"David!" I called out.

Silence.

The isolation of the woods, once peaceful, now felt unsettling as I stood still, trying to figure out what to do. With no cell service to call him, I decided to follow the path that made more sense, hoping he would turn around soon. Panic started to arise.

"DAVID!!" I yelled again, but much louder. Still nothing.

He won't go far before he realizes you're not right behind him.

I pedaled forward down the path, frantically looking for him. The other riders were so spaced out that I didn't know how long it would take before someone else came by, and if I took a wrong turn then no one would see me.

"DAVID!!!!" I screamed, a third time.

"WHAT??" he yelled, getting closer to me.

Whew.

I continued toward the sound of his voice until I made a couple more turns and came upon him.

"I thought you were right behind me!" he cried.

"Well, I *was*! I should've downloaded the map!"

Shortly after winding through a few more shaded turns, we came to an opening with a huge, serene pond.

"I have to take a picture!" I said and stopped to pull out my phone from my pack.

This is so nice, enjoying the ride, taking in the scenery, and not worrying about times or pace. This is why I wanted to do this event; for the experience.

"Are you ready for the massive incline ahead?"

"Ugh. NO!" I whined.

The information about the race and multiple e-mails stressed the intensity of the last incline, and the funniest part was that they apologized for it on more than one occasion. In the last mile, there was a 300-meter section at an average of 12% incline with peaks of over 15%, followed by a 6% incline the final 600 meters before leveling out slightly to the finish line. Many cyclists ended up getting off their bikes and walking up the first section, and I was about to find out why.

After taking a hard right turn, I saw it ahead and cried out some choice words that I was thankful no young children were anywhere nearby. Through all the other inclines on the route, I had stayed on my bike, standing up to push the pedals with all my body weight and strength. As I attempted to do this going up a sandy version of Mount Everest, the tires slipped under the soft sand, the pedals locked up, and I toppled over. I pulled my left foot off the pedal just in time to prevent a full face-plant into the dirt and hopped off the bike to walk it up the insane hill.

Nope, not today.

Do what you gotta do to finish.

David was ahead of me and pushed through the incline without getting off his bike. *Show-off.* I saw a truck parked off the side of the trail and realized it was the photographer. He saw me, then grabbed his massive camera and aimed it right at me.

"I heard you would be up here taking pictures of us on the most brutal part of the route, that's pretty messed up!" I laughed.

"This is the best part of the course to take pictures!" he exclaimed with a smile.

I posed in my typical race fashion, flashing a big smile to fake it until I could make it. I continued walking in a hunched-over position, pushing hard to get my bike past the Seventh Circle of Hell. After I passed the photographer, I noticed the shift of the incline drop down to 6% and was relieved to get back on my bike.

I can push my pedals through this.

"That was BRUTAL!!" David cried up ahead, waiting for me to catch up to him.

"Tell me about it, I had to walk!"

We pushed up the last part of the less intense incline, and I could see the skies part over the finish line about a quarter mile ahead. We picked up speed and rode side by side as we approached the finish. The announcer saw us coming, and called out through the speaker, "Are y'all gonna sprint to the end?!"

I took the bait, stood up on my pedals, and cycled ferociously through the finish line, cackling like a witch flying on her broomstick. About a dozen people were hanging out under the large tent, cheering and laughing as my inner child emerged and I squealed going through the finish line. David didn't fall for it and casually rode through right after me; I was the sucker. The announcer laughed and called out our names.

We took our bikes to the car, loaded them up on the rack, and headed back over to the tent to get some water and wait for the other cyclists to finish. I couldn't wait to see the winners from the 45-mile race come in. I saw a couple of ladies working the event and walked up to them to ask when the riders typically finished. She said they would be there in the next thirty minutes, so we decided to stick around.

"We usually run road races, so this is our first time doing this," I explained.

"So, if y'all are runners, what brought you here?"

"We wanted to try something new and different, and absolutely loved it!"

"That's great, we're so glad you're out here today!" she beamed.

Oddly enough, one of the last things I want to do after completing a race is to sit down. Even if I'm standing or slowly walking, it feels better to keep an easy momentum going while my body cools down. Once I sit, it's like my butt sinks into a sandpit and I struggle to get up. I also didn't have a desire to put my bottom on any kind of surface for a few minutes if I didn't have to. David ate a burrito they had available as a post-race meal, and I had a protein shake and an Aloha Bar.

"You don't want a burrito?" he asked.

"Of course, I *want* a burrito, but unfortunately I have no idea what it would do to my stomach."

It was right around thirty minutes when first place for the 45-mile race came in. There was a slight hill of the trail that was a quarter mile away, visible from where we were waiting, so I kept a close eye out.

"There he is!" I shouted, then pulled out my phone and ran to the edge of the trail about 100 feet past the finish line to take a video of him coming in. I am rarely able to witness first place finishing at a race, and I was beside myself with excitement.

"Wow, he is bookin' it!" David exclaimed.

He sure was. The announcer called out his name and said that he was in first place as he soared through the finish line. Right after he passed me, he veered off to the right, hit the brakes, and collapsed onto the ground. I gasped.

Oh my gosh, is he okay??

His family immediately ran to him with cold bottles of water, standing over and talking to him while he breathed heavily. I watched as his shaky hands reached up and unzipped his jersey to help cool off.

"Oh, wow," David said, standing next to me.

We watched as second, third, and fourth places came in, somewhat spaced apart by about a minute each. They came to a stop, standing there and talking to each other while the guy in first place was still lying on the ground, getting himself together. After a couple of minutes, he got up and started walking around, his family placing water cloths on his neck and chest.

"Wow, he really wanted first place!" David said.

"No kidding! Well, if he pushed that hard, he certainly deserved it!"

"Yes, he did!"

We stayed for a few more minutes, then decided to hit the road to make the hour-and-a-half drive back home. He triple-checked the bikes fastened to the rack before we left, then stopped again before we hopped on the interstate. We didn't want a repeat on our way home.

"I am so glad you talked me into doing this race, it was great!" he said as we rode down the interstate.

"I loved it, I felt so connected with nature!"

"You know, I kind of hoped you wouldn't want to do this race, but I'm really glad you got us out here. We should get gravel bikes and do the 45-mile route next time!"

"Whoa, slow your roll, Rocky. I won't be ready for something that far for a while."

"I'm not saying do it right now, but we need to do it! I'm going to look at gravel bikes when we get home, and definitely need to get a better bike rack. I don't want that ever happening again."

Uh oh, I think I created a monster.

Y'all can be monstrous together.

I told him about the conversation with the ladies earlier, asking me why we decided to do a bike race since we were runners.

"I don't want to be limited to *just* running. There's no reason we can't try different endurance events and other activities, whether it's off-road cycling, trail runs, duathlons, triathlons, swimming, road races, pickleball, soap carving, basketweaving, gardening, whatever! I want to try them all to experience what each one has to offer, mix things up, see what I like and don't like, and don't want to be tied down to just *one* activity with these races," I babbled.

"I agree, I want to try more events, too."

I texted pictures before and after the race to my family, telling them the ride was much harder than I expected it to be.

"Have fun!" said my mom.

"Good luck!" Michael chimed in.

"Wait until you hit 50!" my dad retorted.

"This bike ride will be easy when I'm 50!" I said.

"Yeah, sure."

"Wanna bet?"

Silence.

Maybe he knows that betting against me would be a bad idea; especially now.

He was just trying to be funny; you're overthinking this.

I probably am. I know his intentions are good, but I have already wasted so much time with a fixed mindset that has held me back. Not anymore.

One of my favorite things to look up after races is the oldest age of competitors. In our 13-mile race, the youngest was 40 and the oldest was 67. The irony was that we finished almost last! Well, David could have finished closer to the front if he hadn't stayed with me, so he was stuck with a giant toddler. The oldest competitor in the 45-mile race was 76: my dad's age.

The more I thought about it, the more determined I became. I had seen an incredible number of people in their seventies and even eighties in multiple races, and I want to be like them when I reach that age.

The more that people have doubted me, the more I have committed to never giving up, driven by the desire to show *myself* that I was capable of achieving new goals. Their fixed mindset and doubt became a fire behind my motivation to push me beyond what I thought was possible. Fortunately, Michael had even shifted, and I could only hope that my slapping him with unexpected accomplishments has been a contribution to thinking outside the box.

Maybe one day he'll try something new, too.

Lead by example, be a positive influence, and stay in your lane.

Before I started running, I had viewed aging as myself becoming a feeble old lady sitting on the front porch in a rocking chair, drinking sweet tea, and yelling at squirrels stealing food from the bird feeder. I figured it was my fate and was afraid of what the future held.

I want to be strong and active as I age for as long as possible. I don't want to be a porch ornament.

You don't have control over aging, but you do have some control over HOW you age.

I refuse to spend the rest of my life seeing challenges as obstacles instead of opportunities to

grow. I want to struggle. I want to fail. I want to overcome adversities. Nothing in life worth having comes easily, and I want to work hard to earn my accomplishments.
That's called a growth mindset.

Struggling up the 15% incline with a smile.

-29-

WEATHERING THE STORM

"Well, it looks like there's no school tomorrow with Hurricane Helene coming through. I guess the weather is supposed to get pretty terrible for them to cancel altogether," I said to David while looking at the upcoming weather forecast on a Thursday evening.

The main reason they cancel school in our district is based on transportation issues, as buses are unable to reach certain parts of the county. Fortunately, we live close to our kids' schools and can drive to them in just a few minutes. Kaitlyn and Alex were excited to be able to sleep in the next morning, so we relaxed and let them stay up a little later than usual. I was slacking on my Sleep Police duties.

The next morning at 3:30 am, the deep quiet of the night was interrupted by a sudden violent rainstorm that jolted us awake. Flying debris battered against the house, rain pounded relentlessly on the windows, and the wind seemed to shake the entire house. The noise grew more intense, and David got out of bed to look out the window into the darkness as I lay there in shock at the intensity.

"It would be a miracle if we didn't lose power," he said as he returned to bed.

It seemed to relax just a little, enough for me to fall back asleep for an hour before it came back even harder and more severe. At 5:30 a.m., the lights flickered, then everything went black.

Oh, great. Hopefully, it won't be out long.

David had gotten up just a few minutes before, unable to go back to sleep. The noise outside grew louder, and my heart beat faster with it. I could hear the trees swaying violently, their branches creaking and snapping under the force of the wind. Panic started to arise when I thought of Alex sleeping on the top floor of the house, and one of the enormous pine trees crashing down on the roof.

What if a tree falls on his bedroom?

That's unlikely, but it couldn't hurt to go ahead and get up to check on him.

As I walked into the hallway, Kaitlyn came out of her room, terrified of the storm. The hum of electricity that we didn't even realize was so comforting was gone, leaving the house eerily quiet except for the intensity of the storm outside. David and Alex were armed with flashlights and lanterns in the living room. You know it's a bad storm when the kids can't sleep through it. We stared out the windows in the darkness, unable to see what was happening outside.

As the sun started coming up, we were able to slowly see some of the debris in the yard. It looked like there was a college-style party during the night, with both lounge chairs in the pool, and our outdoor sofa set strewn into the neighbor's yard next door, along with the pool toys scattered everywhere. There was no telling what we didn't notice that had gone missing and ended up in another neighbor's grass like an unwrapped Christmas present. The yard looked as if the trees drank too much and threw up all over the front and back yard, with branches, bushes, leaves, pine straw, and pinecones everywhere we looked. My mom sent me a picture of their neighbor's covered boat dock, which had completely broken away from the rest of the dock and was nestled up against their seawall. The worst was yet to come.

"We lost a *huge* tree in our yard," Michael said when he called shortly after sunrise. "Thankfully, it fell toward the road, because if it had fallen on the house, it would have landed over my bedroom."

In Aiken, David's cousin, Katie, along with her husband and 1-year-old son stayed at her uncle's house. Three doors down from her uncle, a tree fell on a couple's home and killed them both. When Katie went home, she discovered that two trees had fallen on her home and destroyed it: one directly over her baby's room. Andrew's childhood friend's dad was tragically killed by a tree that landed on his firetruck that morning while headed out for an emergency to help others in need. My heart was broken for his wife and son; they were some of the nicest people I had ever met. South Carolina had the most power outages of any other state in the Southeast, and the flash flooding in Western North Carolina was devastation that no one had expected or experienced.

"Do y'all have power?" my mom asked when she called after the sun came up. We always check in with each other during storms, especially since they live right down the street from us.

"No, but David hooked the generator up to the coffee maker, so we can function through this chaos!"

"Oh, you have *coffee*?!"

A few minutes later, she and my dad showed up to share in the indulgence and discuss the enormity of the storm and its impact on the area. When Michael had called while he was riding from his house to our house, I heard the shock in his voice as he reported how many trees had fallen on Hwy 378, obliterating power lines as far as the eye could see. Being closer to downtown, Robbie never lost power, but his yard was destroyed by fallen trees and huge branches.

"I would be shocked if we got power back by tonight," David said.

"Don't say that! I hope it won't be that long!"

As the day went on, panic started to arise over how much food I had stored in our refrigerators and freezers. Yes, plural for both. As a chef, I do a lot of meal prep and keep our freezers stocked with meal options, so I don't have to cook everything from scratch at every meal. David set up the generator to run one refrigerator/freezer and our standup freezer, so it allowed me to declutter what food we didn't need and store the good stuff to keep it from spoiling.

That night, the four of us piled into the guest bedroom in the basement with a window unit air conditioner hooked up to the generator. Our generator was small and could only power a few things, so we used it wisely. During the first part of the day, I was annoyed and stressed over losing power, but the more I learned about what so many others had experienced, I felt grateful for what we had when I laid down to go to bed that night. We had each other. We had a home. We had food and water. We had what we truly needed to make it through the storm. The next day, I received a phone call from my mom, and I could tell she had been crying. She called to tell me that my cousin, her brother's daughter, had passed away at the age of 50 from bone cancer. It happened very quickly, in a matter of weeks, and hit all of us hard that she was gone in what seemed an instant. My heart hurt terribly for my aunt, uncle, and cousins who suffered the most from the loss of her.

For the following three days, each morning looked the same with my mom coming over to have coffee with us, taking some back for my dad. He prefers instant coffee, so once they were able to utilize their hot plate to boil water, he started enjoying his fake coffee at home. Ever since David started ordering good quality coffee beans and grinding them for our daily pot, we had become spoiled rotten.

Over the weekend, I had somewhat adjusted to not having power, with us camping out in the basement bedroom and doing whatever we could during the day to keep ourselves occupied. Alex had a tough time with not having internet, which made me realize how dependent he was on it. I watched in horror as he tried to "fix" the modem multiple times in an attempt to restore the precious internet.

"He's like a little monster without the internet!" I said to David. "This is not healthy; we need to pull back on screens more!"

When Monday came, the house felt hotter than it had all weekend. We couldn't leave the sliding glass doors open because the animals would get out and didn't have screens over the windows to be able to open them for fresh air without a swarm of bugs making themselves at home. I felt like I was hitting an emotional breaking point and needed to get outside in the neighborhood for a walk by myself.

"Can I come with you?" Kaitlyn asked.

"Not this time."

"Why not?" she whined.

"Mom needs some time to herself," David said. *This man knows me very well.*

"Yes, I do. I'm sorry, but I really need to go for a walk by myself right now."

"But *why*? I want to go!"

"I said no."

Although part of me felt guilty, I also knew what I needed desperately at that moment. If I didn't get a break to take a little time for myself, my mood would only get worse. My patience would be even thinner, and I was quickly running out of *nice* energy. David and the kids had spent the weekend getting out of the house regularly, between going to the store, riding around, and going to Aiken to help his parents. He didn't feel comfortable running the generator while no one was there, so I stayed behind for them to go. After going for a walk, I felt a little better, but still needed to at least get out of our neighborhood and knew that both of my brothers had power.

"I have got to get out of here, I'm going over to Michael's house for a couple of hours."

"Why?" David asked.

"Being trapped in this stuffy, hot house is starting to wear on me."

"It's hot for us too, it's not all about you."

I felt anger arise and knew immediately that I needed to leave before I said something without thinking first. After I dropped Alex off at his friend's house for a playdate (they had power), I drove to Michael's house. I walked in and felt relief being somewhere that had lights, air conditioning, and internet. I plopped myself into the recliner and pulled out my laptop to work on some coloring books and cookbooks for the upcoming holidays. Tracy walked out of her office to say hello and see how everything was going.

"I had to get out of there, I was trapped all weekend and needed a break...with some air! David and the kids can handle the heat better than I can, especially with this perimenopause crap!"

"Trust me, I know all about that!" she laughed.

Sometimes, family members have a hard time understanding the hormonal changes women go through, especially as we enter this phase. I stayed there for an hour to decompress, then hopped in the car to head home. On my way there, Kaitlyn called.

"WE HAVE POWER!!" both she and David cheered through the phone.

"Wait, are you serious? Don't play with my emotions right now! Do we *really*?!"

"YES!!"

My shoulders relaxed with a feeling of relief, and I felt like 40 pounds magically disappeared from my shoulders. I wanted to cheer. I wanted to cry. But most of all, I felt relieved, and a feeling of calmness engulfed me. We had gone 82 hours without power, and now it was restored.

"Are you alright?" he asked when I walked in.

"I'm sorry, I hit a breaking point earlier, and I got upset when you said this wasn't all about me. I have never thought this was all about me and have been home all weekend while y'all got out and went different places. The heat has been climbing in this house, and I just needed a break. My heart has felt so much pain empathizing with the people who are truly suffering, and the emotional weight has felt very heavy."

"It seemed like it came out of nowhere, and I have been stressed too with missing work on top of dealing with everything."

"I know you have, and this didn't come out of nowhere for me. I had been struggling for several days but was doing everything I could to stay strong for you and the kids, and my heart hurt deeply for so many people. That's the hardest part of being an empath, *feeling* other people's pain. I was already so grateful and appreciative for what we have, especially considering what everyone else has gone through this weekend and I had a moment of weakness."

"No one is perfect, and no one will ever be perfect. I know you don't think it's all about you, it's been stressful for everyone, but now we have power and can move forward!"

"I have never been so thankful for electricity in my life," I smiled and rested my head on his shoulder.

When the power was restored, the air relaxed at home. Meanwhile, the devastation in Western North Carolina continued to grow, and we were heartbroken at the damage we saw. Asheville is our favorite place to visit in North Carolina, and we stared in shock as the damage and death toll grew. As the floods came down the mountain, downtown Columbia and Cayce were in danger of flooding, and many people had to evacuate their homes until the water levels decreased to safety. Our kids were out of school for a few days, so it was a relief when we received the information about them going back. Alex was excited, while Kaitlyn was not. David and I were both elated for all of us to resume some normalcy and be on a schedule again.

The following Saturday, Alex and I wore yellow to run a 5k in honor of my cousin's passing. Although we weren't super close growing up, I always respected and looked up to her in many ways. She was abnormally intelligent, with a bright smile, a great sense of humor, and a contagious laugh. She was strong, independent, and a fighter who didn't give up easily on challenges in life. She and one of my closest childhood friends, Kari, shared so many of the same characteristics and always reminded me of each other, which drew me to her.

As I ran the race, I thought about her and felt like I was carrying her spirit with me, step by step. It felt like a chance to honor the life she couldn't live anymore. She wasn't a runner, but I felt sure in my heart that she would have been out there walking if she *could*.

That day, I started running for those whose bodies won't let them, whose hearts or health hold them back from feeling the rush of the wind and the rhythm of the road. Every step is a reminder of the gift of movement, of a freedom not everyone has. They inspire me to keep going, to push through the discomfort because I can. I started to dedicate the strength of my legs to those who couldn't be out there alongside me, adding more fuel to the motivation to continue moving forward.

Rest In Peace, Julie.

-30-

FULL CIRCLE

It had been exactly twelve years since my emotional dumpster fire attempt to run the school Run Hard 5k in November 2012 with my 9-year-old nephew, Andrew. Only this time, it was with my 9-year-old son, Alex. There was no doubt whether I could run the entire distance, the question was if I could *stay* with him. David was also running with us and was faster than Alex, so I knew that even if I couldn't keep up with them, he was still with an adult. I didn't have my own race bib with a chip that recorded my time. I didn't have a personal record to break. I didn't have any chance of placing in my age group or standing on a podium. My personal goal was to do my best to keep up with my favorite boys and see what my mind and heart were capable of on top of my developed fitness capacity.

I also wanted to show Alex the importance of persevering and not giving up on your goals in life. How important it is to be consistent. How important it is to stick with something even if it doesn't come naturally to you, and to have a positive mindset. I felt confident it wouldn't be an emotional dumpster fire like it was twelve years ago, but it was also an opportunity to see what I was made of, even if it was just a 5k. I wanted to teach our kids to grow up with a growth mindset, instead of having to change later in life like I had to do.

One week before the race, we participated in the Run Hard community event, with the Half-Marathon, 10k, and 5k distances that we had done every year. David had developed a nasty cold but still planned on running the Half-Marathon distance while Alex and I did the 5k.

"Are you sure about this? You know you can drop down to the 10k or 5k."

"I'm not dropping down, I'll be fine."

Mmm-kay.

When we lined up for our race, I looked around to see if I recognized any of the other runners. I did a double take when I saw a guy who looked exactly like one of Michael's close childhood friends but shook my head at the thought.

No way. That's not Jaye, he would NEVER be out here running a 5k. Not a chance.

I had invited another mom from the after-school program to do the race with me since Alex was running with Zack. Stephanie and I clicked at practice after she joked that her mid-life crisis was running. She had also never been a distance runner, but she progressed significantly faster than I had and already beat my personal best time in just a few short months, even though I had been running for 2 ½ years. At first, I started to think it was more proof that solidified I truly wasn't a natural at distance running, but my intuition stepped in and reminded me that we're all different, and I enjoyed being around her. My soul trumped my ego.

About a mile into the race, the guy I saw slowly passed me, so I called out his name to see if he would turn around, and he did. It really was him.

"What are *YOU* doing here?!" I cried, shocked.

"I had a heart scare a few months ago, so I started running. I'll tell you about it after because I can't really carry on a conversation right now!" he laughed and pushed forward.

"Go get it!" I cheered and smiled.

Stephanie and I stayed together most of the route but had different strengths. My endurance had developed enough to keep a steady pace the entire distance, but she was faster than me between her walk and run intervals. She plugged ahead in the last mile and ended up beating me by a minute. The fastest runners in the area participated in either the Half-Marathon or 10k, so she was floored when I pulled up the results and told her she placed first in our age group, and I got second. We were beside ourselves with excitement to stand on the podium next to each other.

I don't care that she beat me, I'm SO happy she came out here today! She has a lot of potential, and I'm going to continue encouraging her!

I met up with Jaye and his wife, Melanie, after the race to get the details on why he started drinking the running Crazy Juice.

"Well, one day I started having this really weird lightheadedness, nausea, and numbness in my hands after I was working hard out in the yard, so I went to Urgent Care. They couldn't find anything at that moment and referred me to a cardiologist, and he told me that I needed to start exercising and drinking more water, so I did, and here I am!"

"Well, you certainly have a reason to stick around for a *very* long time!" I smiled as I patted his wife's pregnant belly.

Only three miles into his race, David realized he should have stayed home to rest and recover from his cold...but he pushed through the entire 13.1 miles. His illness plummeted over the next few days, with his cold going into his chest, and it sounded like he was an 85-year-old man hacking up a lung with each cough.

"Are you gonna make it?" I asked, concerned. That's the usual question we ask each other when one of us is struggling.

"Ugh," he responded.

Race day came, and I was both nervous and excited. Alex had improved from the previous seasons in the Run Hard program and moved up to the first corral with the faster runners. My mind wandered as I stared out the window of the car on our way to Alex's school event that morning. I couldn't wait to see what he could do, but started to doubt what I could do.

Can I keep up with him? I may be able to run much better than I did twelve years ago with Andrew, but Alex is quite fast. His personal best 5k time is 3 minutes faster than I have ever run. He is a natural endurance athlete like David, and I have to work at least three times as hard as them.

You don't know if you don't try.

"Are you running with us?" David asked.

"I'm going to try!"

"Yeah Mommy, run with us!" Alex cheered.

"I'm going to *really* do my best and give everything I've got to keep up with y'all today."

"Okay," Alex paused and thought for a second. "Well, I can slow down so you can keep up with us."

My heart melted, and I smiled at his kindness.

"Thank you, I appreciate it...but I want you to do your best today. This is *your* race!"

Arriving at the Columbiana Mall in Irmo looked like it did in the Spring, with a massive amount of cars invading the parking lots, swarming in like bees taking over a hive. It was chilly, so we were bundled up in pants and pullovers until it was time to strip down and run. Over 1,000 kids lined up in their corrals by the start line with their buddy runners...so there were over 2,000 people running. Coach Jesse gave everyone words of encouragement before he unleashed the madness in waves, with many kids taking off at full speed, and a few of them even took a spill right out of the gate because they were running too fast.

When we took off, David and Alex were right behind me as we crossed the start line. I turned on my Bluetooth speaker attached to my pants pocket and started my race playlist. The kids loved it at after school practices when I ran with music playing, so I made sure to bring it along for the event. Not long after we started, my boys passed me...quickly.

Oh my gosh, they're moving really fast!

Pick up your speed and try to keep up with them for as long as possible.

I sped up, keeping them in my sight just ahead of me as we moved swiftly with the crowd. We continued along the road circling the mall, and they slowly started inching ahead. About a half mile in, they broke away too far ahead for me to keep up with them any longer.

You're on a different path than Alex, and you have come so far from where you started. Focus on doing YOUR best.

I smiled as I watched them disappear in the crowd ahead, excited to see what he could do and focused on my pace and breathing. I hadn't run at all since the previous 5k one week ago, and my body was struggling to warm up in the cold weather. I got into a rhythm with my legs pumping along steadily, and it didn't take long for me to roll up my long sleeves I wore under the Run Hard race shirt. When Coach Dave presented the new Run Hard mascot at the beginning of the season at our school, I couldn't help but to smile. Tank the Tortoise represented the program, signifying how although the tortoise moved slowly, he never gave up. It couldn't describe my own personal path more perfectly, and I loved how they put it in this perspective for the kids as well, focusing on effort over perfection.

After we circled the mall and made our way out to the surrounding neighborhood, my body started to really feel warmed up. Approaching mile 1, I thought about my pace and wondered how well I could do on my time for one mile.

"There's the 1-mile marker!" I heard a dad beside me shout to his daughter running next to him.

It was closer than I expected and passed the sign quickly as I looked down to see my time.

Oh my gosh! That is the fastest mile I have ever run in my life at 9:10! I can't believe it!!

Look; your fastest mile at the age of 44. Pat yourself on the back for that one!

As I ran deeper into the neighborhood, the hills started coming out of nowhere like waves in the ocean. The first mile of the course was pretty flat, but the second mile had some inclines that I wasn't expecting.

Yikes, this is challenging.
You've got this, just stay steady. You don't have to run fast, just keep going.

I plugged along, listening to the music on my playlist. We approached the edge of the neighborhood and made it back to the main road running next to the mall, and it was lined with spectators cheering for the runners as we passed by. I scanned the crowd, spotting several familiar faces and smiled as I saw them.

My favorite motivational song, *Born For This* by The Score, came blaring through my speaker. Between the energy of the people surrounding me and sinking deeply into the lyrics, the timing was perfect as I listened carefully to the words.

We are the broken ones,
Who chose to spark a flame
Watch as our fire rages,
Our hearts are never tame
'Cause we were born for this

I thought about how I was so emotionally broken the first time I attempted the 5k with my nephew 12 years ago. I thought about how the fire had been ignited in my heart and soul since I started running and got excited moving forward to see what's in store for the future.

I've struggled for years and
Through all of the tears
I've faced the doubts I hide
I never gave into my fears deep within
'Cause I heard my voice inside
I know, I was born for this

I thought about how much I held myself back throughout my life with self-doubt, fears, and a fixed mindset I didn't realize I had; yet still knew deep down there was a fire within me that hadn't yet been ignited.

I believe, I believe
We can write our story
I believe, I believe
We can be an army

I thought about how the choices I make are what largely determine my future and path ahead. If I choose to make choices that only satisfy instant gratification instead of the long road ahead, I will pay the consequences for it.

These words that I write
Are for someone like me
To know you're not alone
The moves that you make
Yeah they come with mistakes
Don't ever lose your hope
Just know, you were born for this

Goosebumps arose on my arms as I really listened to these words, reminding me to focus on doing the best I can do in *every* aspect of my life. You might want to argue that the goosebumps came from the weather, but by this point I was hot, sweaty, and a complete emotional puddle of goo by getting so engulfed in a song. But, like I mentioned earlier, music takes me places emotionally that I could never fully explain.

We turned back onto the road going back into the mall, and I could see the finish line a quarter mile away. My face spread into a smile, with a sense of overwhelming joy as I continued to run. Coach Gary was up ahead, with his famous "Power Up" station, cheering us on. He's out there at every Run Hard school race, close to the finish line. As you run by, you fist bump or high five these large, flat, round discs he's holding up for you to get a dose of "power" as you approach the end. I smiled as I ran by and slapped it, laughing and speeding up for the final turn down the chute to the finish.

I made the last turn and sprinted, along with some of the other parents, coaches, and kids as we all completed the race and had a huge smile on my face. I had read about experienced runners who viewed people sprinting through the finish line of an endurance race as being silly. I could only imagine how a centaur would feel, watching a slow-moving tortoise kick it into high gear when they've been moving at a geriatric speed all along, then gunning for the finish like they ran faster than anyone else.

Well, I am one of those silly tortoises.

When I first started completing races, the *last* thing I was able to do was sprint at the end. It was just a fallacy, a wild dream to be able to run *fast* after 3.1 miles. Honestly, I had already been giving it everything I had just to be able to keep a steady jog the entire time, so dashing at that point seemed ludicrous. As time went on, my endurance and strength built from consistent training, and when I realized I was *able* to sprint at the end…I did it without even thinking (or even caring) what other people thought about me darting through that finish line. I wasn't there to impress them; I was there to test my own limits and capabilities…and have fun while doing it. Sprinting at the end of a race has become a necessity, because I know that I have worked so hard to get to where I am from where I started. I may start out as a tortoise, but eventually morph into a hare.

As I wandered around searching for my family, my mind drifted to the achievements.

-I ran my fastest mile ever, ran another 2.1 miles after it *and* was able to sprint through the finish line.

-I didn't have any bladder leakage (*always a win*).

-I was able to participate in an event for a program that holds so near and dear to my heart and has been a large part of my own journey as well as Alex's beginning.

Watching my son see what he was capable of achieving was far better than being able to keep up with him, especially since it came more naturally to him than it did for me. He got his Daddy's centaur genetics. There were no negative thoughts, sadness, or disappointment when I finished, there was only pure joy. I had conquered the abusive inner voice that had caused so much emotional turmoil throughout my life. It was gone, and I was *never* letting it come back. I smiled up at the sun, and random tears of joy trickled down my face as I took in the moment. Shifting my mindset later in life was a far more daunting accomplishment than running a 5k, Triathlon, or Half-Marathon. Challenges stopped being walls I slammed into and became doors I was curious to open. It was an exhilarating sense of possibility, where setbacks became speed bumps, not stop signs. The new perspective breathed life into my everyday routines—failures didn't sting as much, and successes, however small, felt like reasons to celebrate. Each step forward built a sense of accomplishment because I was no longer confined by what I thought I "should" be able to do; instead, I started discovering what I *could* do.

You just wait...this is only the beginning.

Standing on the podium with Stephanie. She kept saying I let her win, but honestly, I was just trying to keep up with her...and failed miserably.

Alex was forced to take a picture with Mom. Poor guy.

-31-

TOMORROW IS AN ADVENTURE

The day after Alex's Run Hard 5k, David and I rolled out of bed as the sun came up and made our way into the living room with the dogs excitedly following us, hoping they would get their breakfast early. We typically make them wait until around 7:00 am so they won't harass us first thing, but they can't seem to help themselves. He made a pot of coffee while I filled a glass of water and immersed myself on the couch, underneath a blanket and pillow on my lap. I usually check e-mail on my phone in the morning, but I was on a mission.

It's time to start planning out goals for next year. Let's look at some races.

I popped open the laptop and immediately went to my favorite race website; runningintheusa.com to browse the selection. It includes all race distances including trail runs, marathons, and even ultras around the country. It also includes multi-sport races like Duathlons and Triathlons. I had become interested in trying some more off-road races.

Since David and I did our first gravel bike race, he became obsessed and bought us beginner gravel bikes. The timing was perfect, since the Osteoarthritis in my hip started acting up again, and I realized that I had to face the reality of adjusting my training. It didn't mean that I had to stop running altogether, it just meant that I needed to train differently, shortening my runs and spending more time cross-training.

This is part of your aging process now, so do what you can, and tweak as needed. This is a good time to start focusing on more triathlons, gravel bike races, and pickleball.

My love for all races had deepened to the point where I wanted to do one almost every weekend and enjoyed mixing it up with a variety instead of just running a local 5k every Saturday. I had been babbling to David a lot about destination races.

"Come on, it's a win-win! We love to travel, get to check out places we've never been, *and* we get to participate in a race! We know from experience that when you run a race route, you get to see the area from a whole different perspective!" I said with spirit and gusto.

"Mm-hmm," he responded.

His coffee hadn't transformed him into a human yet, so I went back to searching the site and made mental notes, adding them to the calendar on my phone, *just in case*. I know him. I know when the gears are turning, especially when I find an event he would be interested in.

"Are you training for any upcoming races?" I texted my old college friend, Chris. He's from Long Island, New York, and moved back after graduating from Coastal Carolina University. In 2015, he rescued an 11-year-old girl from drowning in the ocean. A dangerous riptide swept her and her sister about 100 yards off the shoreline. Chris was working for the Marine Bureau of the Suffolk County Police Department and was at the right place at the right time. He dove into the water, swam out to her quickly, and pulled her to safety; saving her life. A hundred-yard swim was easy for him, even in rough conditions. He has completed multiple marathons, Ironman Triathlons, and has traveled to many different states. Whenever I'm looking for destination races, I reach out to him for suggestions.

"I'm looking at some Half-Ironman Triathlons up here, but I haven't picked one out yet. I also like the one in Augusta, Georgia. My favorite marathon is the Rock 'n Roll Marathon in Nashville, you have to try that one!"

"If you do the one in Augusta, I will come watch."

"If I do it, then you better!"

"Don't put that idea in my brain, I'm crazy enough to consider it!"

I started looking around at different triathlons and looked up the Half-Ironman Triathlon, which is a 1.2-mile swim, 56-mile bike ride, and a 13.1-mile run. This wasn't the first time I had researched the event with different locations, but it also wasn't the first time I felt a strong sense of panic and was overwhelmed just thinking about attempting that far of a distance; especially navigating a modified training schedule with a physical limitation because of my hip.

Could I do a Half-Ironman Triathlon, or have I completely gone off the deep end?

Don't get ahead of yourself, just keep taking baby steps moving forward by trying new races and distances. Don't feel like you HAVE to do it soon, this is a lifelong journey. Enjoy the ride and see where it goes.

The Lake Murray Triathlon in April would be a good one to do since it's a 750-meter lake swim, 16-mile bike, and 5k run; but I'm scared of an open water swim.

Exactly why you should consider it. You won't grow staying inside your comfort zone.

I don't know what the future holds, but I want to continue trying new things; new races, different locations, and different events, to obtain the experience and keep moving forward.

In January of 2024, my best friend was diagnosed with Stage 4 Colon Cancer. To know Virginia is to love her, as she is one of the most incredible people I have ever had the pleasure of having in my life. Since her diagnosis, we have had many deep conversations about what we truly want in life, our goals, and our dreams. This was her second cancer diagnosis, her first being Stage 2 Breast Cancer in 2020. I have always respected her thoughts and opinions since she is so honest and insightful with a strong work ethic and positive attitude, but she developed an even deeper appreciation for life with her experiences. We agreed that finding the balance of both working hard, but still prioritizing time to relax and enjoy life is crucial.

Running opened the floodgates of viewing life through a different lens. It helped me feel better in every way. There's a reason the rearview mirror is much smaller than the windshield in the car. If I keep looking in the rearview mirror, it greatly increases my chances of wrecking what's in front of me. I used to have a strong sense of regret over making mistakes, even though hindsight is 20/20. I started to see mistakes as lessons and experiences that taught me how to grow, even when it was painful. I know that I can't change the past, but I can obtain wisdom from each experience and use that knowledge for the future. That's the best I can do.

Pain helps us grow. Discomfort helps us grow. Trying or learning something new helps us grow. Being challenged by others helps us grow. If we all sat in our recliners and expected life to be easy, we would end up like the people on the giant spaceship in the movie *Wall-E,* floating around on mobile recliners and drinking our meals in the form of milkshakes. David and I laughed when they showed the progression of the generations over the years in that movie. It was funny because it was realistic...and *scary*. We're all human, and we all make mistakes. How we respond to those mistakes is our choice, especially learning from them. I am far from being perfect and still struggle with insecurities and self-doubt, but with a shifted mindset it's easier to navigate the storm when it comes flowing through.

YOU WILL GET THROUGH THIS.

That's my reminder that this too shall pass, and there *is* a light at the end of every tunnel. Although I had developed a love for race events, what I loved most was how my mental, emotional, and physical health had all improved exponentially from making *one* change. That is the beauty of progress over perfection.

The pursuit of perfection is paralyzing, and it used to prevent me from moving forward. Insisting on perfection created unrealistic expectations, and led to devastation when I didn't reach it. Progress is about the journey: the small, incremental steps that lead to improvement over time. By focusing on progress, I allowed myself the grace to make mistakes, embrace imperfections, and learn from setbacks. Failure and struggle eventually became teachers, not an endpoint as I became more resilient; and excited for the future.

Tomorrow is a new adventure, another chance to push beyond the boundaries of what feels safe and familiar. I will continue to step out of my comfort zone, knowing that growth waits on the other side of uncertainty. Each challenge brings a new opportunity to stretch myself and discover strengths I didn't know I had. Stepping into the unknown isn't easy, but that's where the magic of growth lives. With each step forward, I'm reminded that discomfort is just the beginning of something transformative. Tomorrow, I'll embrace the unfamiliar and continue building a stronger, braver version of myself with what little sanity I have left.

First 5k Time: 45(ish) minutes
Personal Best 5K Time: 29:19

-32-

OLD CAR MAINTENANCE

"Getting old sucks!" David cried, frustrated over yet another pulled muscle.

"STOP! You are *not* old!"

"Then why do I get pulled muscles so easily?"

"Have you been doing your strength training and stretching?" I asked. He smiled, which meant no.

"Your body is like a car. As it ages, it requires more maintenance. It's time to get a tune-up," I said.

"I want to trade it in for a new model!"

"Classic cars that are in great condition are more impressive than the new ones! You're not 27 anymore, so you have to take better care of yourself!"

In his twenties and thirties, he could go all out with anything physical and be unaffected by it. These days, a sneeze can lead to whiplash followed by six weeks of physical therapy. I know from my own experience.

Although he cleaned up his diet after being diagnosed with gallbladder disease and experienced major improvements in how he felt, he still needed other tune-ups, like consistent stretching and strengthening. For years, I had experienced constant changes in how my body reacts to almost everything, and I started shifting toward the menopause stage of life with wacky hormones. Every time I thought I figured my body out, something changed.

"But I haven't changed anything," he said.

"That doesn't matter, your *body* changes over time. Think about it; you can't go on a drinking binge all night and work the next day like you could 20 years ago, right? Just because something worked five years ago doesn't mean it will work *now*. Adjust and tweak; that's the best thing you can do as your body shifts."

Wait...did Mr. Logical and I trade places?

NUTRITION AND TRAINING

I've been asked by many people over the years how I lost 50 pounds, so here is a summary. In 2017 after being diagnosed with three digestive disorders and an autoimmune disease, I changed my diet when medications didn't help and have maintained the same weight since May of 2020. I eat a predominantly Mediterranean diet and do daily intermittent fasting of 13-17 hours. I focus on fruits, vegetables, nuts, seeds, legumes, organic lean meats, eggs, and gluten-free whole grains (oats and brown rice). Gluten, dairy, refined sugar, saturated fats, and alcohol are consumed on occasion. I don't eat clean 100% of the time, but I do focus on good quality food that helps fuel my body without making me feel like poo.

Genetic testing informed me that I have a *strong* predisposition for developing Type 2 Diabetes, from both sides of my family and have watched my blood sugar levels slowly creep up over the years. After a ton of research, I learned this can be both prevented *and* reversed through diet and lifestyle. As I age and my hormones shift, I adjust my diet and habits as needed.

I focus mainly on good-quality protein and fiber, and I'm not talking about fiber supplements. I'm referring to *real* fiber, found in food. As women get older, our need for protein and fiber increases. Just in the last year, I have had to make changes and increase protein over carbs (even with running) because my body needs it for building muscle and regulating hormones like insulin and cortisol. When these two hormones are off, they greatly affect my sleep, and I'd prefer not to wake up like the Grim Reaper on a quest for souls to steal. My body functions much better on 3 balanced meals per day, rather than 5-6 smaller meals. I have also noticed a correlation between my Heart Rate Variability and diet, in particular with blood sugar and insulin. If I eat out of balance, my Heart Rate Variability decreases, and fasting helps tremendously. It improves when my diet is more balanced with higher levels of protein and fiber.

Women's bodies also have different needs during their menstrual cycle, balancing intermittent fasting, carbs, protein, and everything in between. Reading *Fast Like A Girl*, by Mindy Pelz, helped me understand why my cravings shifted so much during my cycle, and *Fast.Feast.Repeat* by Gin Stephens is an eye-opening realization on the health benefits of intermittent fasting. Two other books that also greatly helped me understand women's bodies are *Roar* and *The Next Level* by Stacy T. Sims. *It Starts With Food* by Dallas Hartwig and Melissa Hartwig also taught me a lot about regulating insulin and cortisol in the body and finding what works best for ***me***. I could list all of the books I've read over the years, but the page count of this book might put it over the limit for being printed.

For electrolytes, I use Liquid IV and LMNT. The LMNT packets support a fast, so I mix one packet with 20 oz. of water before a long run or race. I save the Liquid IV packets for after since they have a shot of vitamin C and zinc to help my body recover while my immune system is temporarily suppressed. My favorite grab-and-go protein shakes are Orgain Plant-Based Chocolate Protein Shakes, bought in bulk from Costco to save money. The protein powders I use at home are Vega Sport Vanilla and Juice Plus Complete (chocolate and vanilla). I also take Juice Plus capsules, which contain the micronutrients from 30 different fruits and vegetables, and my kids eat the chewables to ensure they get the nutrition as well. I have used a food journal in the past to track my symptoms, IBS flare-ups, and everything else to help figure out what works best for *me*. Remember, I am not a professional athlete, just a middle-aged mom experimenting with what works best for my aging, hormonal, and IBS-infested body.

Although what I have shared works for me at the time being, I also know that my body will continue to shift and change. It's part of the process, and I will make adjustments as needed. When I was younger, I could drink an entire milkshake or eat a plate full of cheese ravioli drowning in alfredo sauce with a side of garlic bread and have no reactions, but these days my belly would be begging for mercy if I decided to throw those into it. Our bodies change. People change. Life changes, so embrace it while you can and learn from it. Like my wise cousin, Aja, says, "It is what it is!" This information I have shared works for me, but that doesn't necessarily mean it will work for *everyone*.

Everybody is different; so, focus on finding what works best for **YOU**! You are unique in your own way, so embrace your weirdness. It makes life more interesting!

My training schedule shifted once I received a diagnosis for my hip, refocusing on strength training to help prevent future injuries. As my healing continues, I will slowly increase the distance for running and cycling sessions. I take it week by week to see what my body can handle until it's ready, and workouts will shift depending on which event I am training for!

I do not do my workouts all at once, I typically break them up into multiple times during the day. My daily schedule is different, but usually, I do runs and cycling that are less than an hour first thing in the morning, while fasted. I don't do strength training workouts fasted, because my body seems to thrive better with this *after* eating.

If my body is worn out, overtired, or sick, I ease up on workouts. When I go on vacation, I still do yoga since I have it on my phone and throw in activities like a run, walk, bike ride, or something active. A total day off is rare when I don't do *anything*, since most of the time if it's a complete rest day I will at least do 30 minutes of yoga or go for an easy walk or run. I stay consistent with yoga, doing this 5-7 times a week for mobility and flexibility, which are crucial for how I feel overall.

When it comes to running, I train both on the treadmill and outside. We have **iFit** on our treadmill and stationary bike at home, and although I was stubborn at first because I claimed I *hated* running on a treadmill, I became hooked after just the first workout. It helped me regulate a steady pace for longer since I was less likely to decrease the speed. It was a mind game. On the treadmill, I'm keeping up with someone else (even if I'm really not) and it's motivation to keep me going. I can also run any time of the day, in any weather as long as we have electricity. When running outside, the fresh air, weather, and music blaring in my ears are refreshing and prepare my body for races since those occur outside, and I can run with someone else. It's a personal preference, and I like to mix it up to get the benefits of both types of training.

My strength training workouts are the Iron Series with Caroline Girvan on YouTube, 21 Day Fix from BeachBody, or sometimes going to the gym. I started out using 8-10 lb. dumbbells, and worked my way up to 15-20 lbs. I love using dumbbells at home and being able to adjust the amount of weight depending on how I feel. Some days when I feel beastly, I'll go for heavier weights. On other days when I feel dainty, I'll go with lighter weights and focus on form. I strength train because I'm not getting any younger and with this pesky perimenopause stealing my muscle and sucking the life out of me, strength training helps me maintain a little sanity, keeps me strong, and helps me look halfway decent in a sleeveless shirt.

Did someone order tickets to the gun show?

Since I started running, the two biggest lessons I learned when it comes to my physical health are to be patient with progression and prioritize strength training. I plan to eventually get to where I can run longer distances, but I learned to have more patience. This is something I want to be able to do for the rest of my life, so it requires making logical decisions and taking my time. Since we fell in love with gravel bike races, we will be cycling more often and increasing our distances. I play pickleball 1-2 times a week because it's fun, and I get to be around people. Pickleball is like Tennis and Ping Pong had a baby. So. Much. Fun.

I enjoy group fitness classes, but since I'm able to force myself to work out at home on my own, it is my best option for maximizing time efficiency since I don't have to drive anywhere. Plus, I tend to socialize a good bit before and after, taking up *more* time. If you're looking for group exercise classes, **ISI Elite** has a group class format that creates a sense of community and accountability, where members encourage and motivate each other. Trained coaches guide every session, and members receive personalized instruction and support. The workouts vary and are challenging, which keeps things exciting and helps members see consistent progress. **Hotworx** consists of 15–45-minute sauna workout sessions that are phenomenal because they combine the benefits of infrared heat with efficient, varied workouts that boost caloric burn, flexibility, and cardiovascular health. It's a unique approach that allows for a comprehensive workout that maximizes results in less time; just be prepared to sweat all the gunk out of your body!

I have trained at both of these facilities and absolutely *love* them, along with several other group fitness classes at regular gyms. There are plenty of places to find group fitness classes if that is your cup of tea, so happy hunting! Find something that you halfway enjoy, and don't be afraid to try out a facility to see if it's the right fit for you.

The bottom line here is: ***strength training is IMPERATIVE for injury prevention!!***

Below is a sample weekly schedule of my training and activities. Always assume I throw 30 minutes of yoga on top of these workouts 5-7 times each week. It adjusts weekly, depending on an event, where I am in my menstrual cycle or life in general. Don't hold me to a strict schedule because you might be disappointed when I say, "Nah, I didn't do that today, I did something else." I love the freedom and listening to my body, so flexibility has been a staple in my schedule.

Monday
-Cycling or Swimming
-Lower body strength training
Tuesday
-Running (3-5 miles)
-Pickleball
Wednesday
-Cycling
-Lower body strength training
Thursday
-Running (3-5 miles)
-Upper body strength training
Friday
-Cycling
-Lower body strength training
Saturday
-Running (long run or race)
-Upper body strength training
Sunday
-Rest

About The Author

In May of 2022, Erin K. Courtney ran a 5k for the first time in her life two months before her 42nd birthday. Although she had previously enjoyed being active, running farther than one block at a time seemed downright ludicrous for a middle-aged mom who had never been a runner. It fueled a fire within her that she never knew existed, shifting her mindset completely and leading her down a path she never thought was possible.

After working in the restaurant industry as a pastry chef, she ventured out into the wild on her own, creating recipes and writing cookbooks for people to make simple recipes in the comfort of their own homes. After being forced to change her diet due to health issues, she became passionate about living a healthy lifestyle and encouraging others to find what is best for them by making small habit changes.

Erin is married to the greatest guy on the planet, they have two ridiculously cute kids and reside in Lexington, South Carolina. After completing certification programs through the Institute of Integrative Nutrition and the Academy of Culinary Nutrition, she hopes to help shed some light and provide inspiration for other people through their own personal health journeys.

I cannot thank you enough for taking the time to read my book, and I truly hope it has inspired you to try something new that you never thought you could accomplish! Most of all, I hope it can somehow help you find a way to your own path. If you could take the time to leave a review, I would greatly appreciate it!

I have made a few videos of the larger races and recipe videos if you want to check them out on my YouTube channel, under Chef Erin's Kitchen. I share more recipes on my website, including the ones mentioned in this book. You can also connect with me on Instagram or Tiktok @cheferincourtney.

www.cheferinskitchen.com

All my books are available on Amazon, scan the QR code below if you would like to check them out, and you can follow my author page to receive updates of newly published books. Thanks again, and don't be afraid to try something new; you may surprise yourself!

E-mail: ekirk713@gmail.com

Made in the USA
Columbia, SC
08 December 2024